GENESIS For Kids

Science experiments that show God's power in Creation!

written by

Doug Lambier and Robert Stevenson

illustrated by Ken Save

Tommy
NELSON™

Thomas Nelson, Inc.
Nashville

Genesis for Kids was written by Robert Stevenson and Doug Lambier and illustrated by Ken Save.

Robert Stevenson

Robert loves being able to draw kids' attention to God through the intricacies of His creation as studied in science. He received his teaching degree at the University of British Columbia and has been teaching science for the past 12 years.

Doug Lambier

Doug's favorite passages in the Bible are chapters 38–41 of the Book of Job where God describes the many wonders of His creation. Doug has been passing on his love of nature and science to his students for the last 8 years. He has a master of science in education degree from the University of Oregon.

Ken Save

Ken has been illustrating for nine years—and loving it. He has illustrated books of the Young Readers Christian Library Series, a number of comic books for D.C. Comics, and Sunday school material. He now works with Lightwave Publishing as part of their artistic team.

For Tommy Nelson™

Managing Editor: Laura Minchew
Project Editor: Beverly Phillips

For Lightwave

Managing Editors: Rick Osborne, Elaine Osborne
Project Editor: Christie Bowler
Graphic Design: Terry Van Roon

LIGHTWAVE
building Christian faith in families

Text and Illustrations
    ©1997 by Lightwave Publishing Inc.

Bible verses marked ICB are from the *International Children's Bible, New Century Version*, copyright 1983, 1986, 1988 by Word Publishing.

ISBN 0–8499–4034–6

Printed in the United States of America

TABLE OF CONTENTS

INTRODUCTION

God the Designer

In the beginning God created . . .

"Dr. Paige, Dr. Paige!"

"What is it, Dr. Lenslo?" Dr. Paige glanced up from her chart at her assistant.

"I've just been reading the first chapter of Genesis, and I've realized some most amazing things!" Dr. Lenslo replied.

"Like what?"

"Like, before there was time, and before there was space, there was God! Before there was light or darkness, God had a plan for everything. Before any creature or other living thing had a place to call home, God knew their needs and made the supplies to provide for them. Before the foundations of the universe were laid, God saw each person and made an incredible plan for their lives."

"That sounds like a great opening for a book!" Dr. Paige exclaimed.

"Hmmm. Interesting idea. Anyhow, doesn't what I've just said flip your cover with excitement?" exclaimed Dr. Lenslo, peering through his telescope.

"It most certainly does!" replied Dr. Paige. "I've been

giving this some thought myself. What God created in each person includes a mind designed to ask questions: Why are we here? How did God make all that we see around us, on Earth and beyond? How do we tackle the problems we see in our world? God invites us to check out all he's placed around us, to step out and try to understand the plans he's had in place all along for the universe and the world we live in. He wants us to know more about his creation!"

"How true, Dr. Paige. God is so big! But he's also interested in the smallest details of the tiniest creatures he placed on Earth. Nothing escapes his attention. He knows everything. He's in everything. His handiwork is displayed in all creation. Every living thing has a place and purpose!" Dr. Lenslo was getting more and more excited. "The balance and patterns in creation show the unchanging nature of our Creator! He is sooooo awesome! I get so focused when I think about this, it makes my head hurt!"

"Now, Dr. Lenslo, don't get so worked up that you crack a lens. Come on! Let's explore the incredible beauty and complexity of God's creation. Let's consider the days of creation, as God reached into the darkness of space and spun our universe into existence—out of nothing! He created a special space around the Earth to make it perfect for life. Using a seemingly endless variety of design, he covered the Earth with plants. He filled the sky with birds and the seas with life. The land was filled with creatures big and small. Then God added his favorite creation: people. Finally, he paused to rest, an activity he knew would be very important for you and me."

"But I don't want to rest right now! There are too many things to explore and investigate. I want to do it all, right now!" proclaimed Dr. Lenslo.

"Pace yourself, my friend. There'll be plenty of time for us to pursue your questions. As the mysteries of God's incredible plan unfold before you, you'll see his hand guiding the formation of the largest galaxies and leading the tiniest creatures to a place of shelter and rest. All creation proclaims the awesome power of the Creator to anyone who will take a few moments to look and listen."

"I wonder how it started? If we study enough, will we be able to do what God did?" Dr. Lenslo asked.

"Well, sometimes things get confused. We're his creation. He is the Creator. We could know all the science ever written or ever thought by the wisest scientists, and still wouldn't be able to do what God did."

Science Is

"Hey! Don't take my word for it," Dr. Paige challenged. "You try what God did. Start with nothing, that's right, nothing, and create everything. Go to the backyard and do some creating. You might want to start with bangs. Bang on something. Go ahead. Make lots of bangs, big ones and little ones. See if you've created some life."

BANG! BANG! Dr. Lenslo banged enthusiastically.

"Does your creation grow, Dr. Lenslo? Does it respond to its surroundings or reproduce?"

Dr. Lenslo looked at what he had produced. Nothing.

"Frustrated?" asked Dr. Paige. "Compare your creation with a simple flower. How many bangs would it take for you to make a flower?"

"Mmmm. I get your point, Dr. Paige. God did something we have no idea how to do."

"Right, you are, my focused friend," Dr. Paige said. "God did something big. Really big. Whatever you think of when you think of God should include the fact that he's no couch potato. God is active . . . he does things."

"He made lots of stuff," mused Dr. Lenslo. "Scientists have a fancy name for that stuff: *matter*."

"Right. When they're not busy inventing names, scientists study matter. They ask questions. They think about matter and do experiments with it. You see, science, too, is active. Science is something you do."

"Wow! I like the doing part of science. Sure beats just reading about it, doesn't it, Dr. Paige?"

"You got a problem with books and reading, Dr. Lenslo?"

"No problem. I've taken a close look at quite a few books."

"I'm thrilled. Hopefully, you've noticed that science is something we all do every day. Every time you wonder why something happens as it does, you're doing science."

"Well, Dr. Paige, I wonder about a lot of things. Like why we wake up with that terrible taste in our mouths."

"Two things: One, you should speak for yourself, and two, this is where science starts . . . with a question. The next step is to guess what the answer might be."

"Okay, Dr. Paige. I'd guess it might have something to do with those late night snacks I enjoy. Nothing like magnified marshmallows smothered in chili sauce and honey."

"Now comes the big leap, my glassy-eyed buddy. Instead of just forgetting about the question or assuming you're right about the snacks, you could design an experiment to put your prediction to the test. That's doing science."

"I'll do it!"

"Good. Start thinking of other questions you'd like answers for. Open your eyes wide and look at everything God put around you. Nothing was put where it is by mistake, including you! As we use science as a tool of discovery, we see so much more about all that God made."

"Science is sooooo awesome!" declared Dr. Lenslo. "Just like God's plans for the world and the universe are ordered by his original design, science helps us bring order to our searching and explorations about creation."

"So pull out your magnifying glass," said Dr. Paige.

"But treat it with special care and attention!" interrupted Dr. Lenslo.

"Definitely! Shift your imagination into high gear. You're about to go on an incredible journey of exploration. Bring some friends along for the trip! Once you've taken a look at some of the ways God's power shows up in creation you'll want to keep going, seeing over and over how his perfect plan is being unfolded around us.

"Science only works because God made it work," Dr. Paige continued. "Matter, light, energy, everything created, only works because God made it work. When you do a science experiment and feel like saying 'Wow!' say an extra thank you for the One who made it all happen. Now. Are you ready to get blown away by our awesome Creator?"

"I was ready before we opened the book!" exclaimed Dr. Lenslo.

Doing Science Safely

We're just about ready to begin, but before we do, a word about this book.

God used a specific order as he created the universe. The Bible tells us he created everything in seven days. We've organized this book in the same way, following the events of Creation. That means we'll discover God's creation in the same order he made it. We'll take a look at what God did on Day 1 and learn about it, then move to Day 2, and so on. With each day we use exciting, fascinating experiments and activities to help us explore our awesome Creator's handiwork.

Just wait until you see what he did!

Now, just like God thought things out carefully, you need to do the same. You have to think and plan so you can do the activities safely. As a scientist working in your home laboratory, there are some very important guidelines you must follow:

1. Some experiments in this book use household chemicals that are poisons if swallowed. The best precaution is to *never taste anything* you're experimenting with unless the instructions tell you to.

2. Always read the entire directions carefully before you start an experiment or activity.

3. Keep things organized. Collect all the tools and materials you'll need before you begin work.

4. Make sure your parents know what you're doing and approve it. They might enjoy doing the experiments with you. Or you could impress them with your scientific knowledge. Try putting on a science show for them after you've practiced a bit!

5. If an experiment calls for using matches, any kind of fire or heat, any kind of household chemicals, or a knife, do that experiment only with adult supervision.

6. When you're finished, put everything back where it belongs, clean up any mess you've made, and wash your hands with soap and water.

7. Be patient. Sometimes results take time.

Are you ready? Here goes!

DAY 1
GOD MADE LIGHT

Genesis 1:3–5: *Then God said, "Let there be light!" And there was light. God saw that the light was good. So he divided the light from the darkness. God named the light "day" and the darkness "night." Evening passed, and morning came. This was the first day.* (ICB)

What happens when someone says "light"? Probably another word pops into your head. Here it comes: "dark." Light and dark. They're opposites. Opposites never spend time together. Oh, it's not that one's good and the other's bad or that they don't like each other. It's just that being seen together is not what being opposites is all about. You'll never see light and darkness together. One always pushes the other out of the way.

Our Earth started in darkness. Perhaps it was resting, getting ready for the busy days ahead. We don't know what it looked like because looking needs light. Of course, there really wasn't anyone to look anyway . . . God hadn't made life yet.

You see, life needs light. So that's where God started. He designed a world with everything necessary for life. Light came first, pushed aside the darkness, and gave us morning.

Light and Dark

Where would we be without *light*? In the *dark*. Try it some moonless night. Get into the dark. Have a buddy lead you (blindfolded, just to be sure) into a room you're unfamiliar with. Observe your surroundings while blindfolded by using your other senses. After all, observation is the basis for all science.

Use your imagination. Pretend your starship *Explorer* just crashed on the gray planet Dark. Your mission is to seek out all life forms and report back to Earth. Careful now, you don't know what lurks in the shadows ahead.

Well . . . what did you observe?

Not much, you say? Exactly. In fact, the experience is almost frightening. In the unfamiliar dark you're likely to trip over something, bump into something, or have some alien jump up and pinch you.

You bumbled around in the dark and found not a speck of life. No green grass or shady trees, no streams full of fish or skies with birds. Not even a spider. Even spiders know better than to hang out on a planet without food. No food? That's right, plants need light to make food. (Learn about food factories in Day 3.)

God made us to live in the light. Light saves us from the experience of darkness. It shows us our surroundings: what we should stay away from and what we should move toward. Light is awesome!

Not everyone can see the light. In fact, even you can't see all of the light that surrounds you. Everyone has "blind spots" in their eyes. Try the following experiment to see how something can become invisible when we look at it from a certain position.

What You Need:
• 2 dimes.
• Eyes.

What You Need To Do:
Place the dimes on a table 3 inches apart. Keep your eyes a foot straight above, and in line with, the dimes. Look down at the left dime with your right eye. Close your left eye. Keep looking at the left dime.

What Do You See?
The right-hand dime disappears! Light lands on the photosensitive cells of the eye's retina to create a nervous impulse to the brain. Presto! Sight! But there are no photosensitive cells where the optic nerve leaves the retina. That's your blind spot. When the light from the right-hand dime lands on this spot it "disappears."

What Is Light?

Have you ever disagreed with someone about something that you were absolutely sure about? Then you discover the person you were disagreeing with was just as sure that he was right? You're not alone. For hundreds of years the big names of science—people like Sir Isaac Newton, James Maxwell, and Albert Einstein—have been arguing about just what *light is*. They each had a theory. And they each were sure they were right. Newton said light was a particle. Maxwell insisted that it was a wave. Then Einstein confused matters by saying it was both.

You are free to take on any of them if you have your own mind made up. If not, keep going: Do some science on the question and come back to it later. You're going to know more tomorrow than you do today. In fact, you're going to keep having questions and keep on learning for the rest of your life.

But about light. The important thing is to realize that God designed light to work in certain ways. Your ability to read words on a page, these words in fact, is proof that light in this room is doing its thing.

"What thing is that," you ask?

Read the answer with our junior scientist.

"Amazing! Electrons in the chemicals that make up the ink on my page are being energized by photons of light that are striking the page. This reflected energy is detected by specialized cells at the back of my eye, the retina. The rod cells of the retina fire corresponding electrochemical signals along the optic nerve to the occipital lobe of my brain. Finally . . . through numerous association pathways in the brain, the little blotches of ink on the page that we call words come to have meaning."

Glad you asked?

That's just the start. There is more to light than what meets your eye.

Double Takes

Everything you observe as a scientist has to be checked out by your brain and *interpreted* before it has meaning. Like this picture. At first you probably only see black dots.

After a while you might see a leopard hidden in the bushes. But think about it; there is no leopard. Not really. The picture is a pattern of dots. You observe that some dots are larger than others, closer together, and so forth. The leopard is in your brain. It's your interpretation of your observation of a pattern of dots. If you had never seen a leopard, you wouldn't be able to interpret the picture.

Why does it matter?

Well, the picture is like a lot of scientific observations: They need to be interpreted. A big part of science experiments is what you do with what you see—how you interpret the evidence.

Your experience affects how you interpret your observations. Say you're awakened very early by strange sounds in your kitchen. Being a scientist at heart, you decide to investigate. You creep into the kitchen and observe your little sister's hand in the cookie jar. Based on your *observations*, you conclude that your little sister is stealing cookies. Right?

Perhaps.

Based on your *experience* of knowing your sister to be honest, you might come to any number of other conclusions. It's possible she was counting the cookies, putting some back, feeling them, or talking to them. Based on your observations alone, you don't really know. It makes you wonder if you can trust what you see.

Good question. Sometimes your eyes play tricks on you. How you interpret what you see can be different from that thing's true measurement, color, depth, or movement. This is called an optical illusion. For instance:

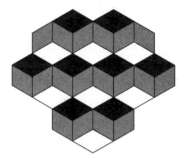

Look at the two figures of circles. The center circle in the figure on the right is larger than the center circle on the left. Right?

Wrong! Both circles are the same size. You see, even though God has given us light to see with, your eyes can play tricks on you.

Which line is longer? Are you sure? Try measuring them. They're even.

Bending Light

Let's take a closer look at light.

What You Need:
- An old tin can.
- A hammer and nail.
- A flashlight.
- A bathroom sink.

What You Need To Do:
With the hammer and nail, poke a small hole in the side of the can near the bottom. Go to the bathroom. Cover the hole in the can with your finger, then fill the can with water. Now turn out the bathroom lights and turn on the flashlight. Point the flashlight down into the can and remove your finger from the hole.

What Do You See?
The beam of light flows inside the water to the basin below. Gravity causes the water to run out of the hole and the light goes with the water. The stream of water acts like a mirror, and you know what happens if you look in a mirror . . . you see your reflection. Lucky you! In this case, it is the beam of light that travels from one end of the stream of water through to the other by a series of internal *reflections*.

This is very similar to the use of light in something called *fiber optics*. You may have seen lamps made of hair-thin glass or plastic strands that carry light from a source in their base through each of the many strands. Think of them as light pipes. Now, what better way to get light into the tiniest of places than to use a skinny bendable light pipe? Need to look inside the motor of a car, or inside someone's stomach? No problem. Send the light in through the light pipe and you know it's going to be reflected back to you along other pipes.

An important everyday use of fiber optics is the carrying of information like computer, television, and telephone data. All of this is the result of light's ability to bounce off things. Perhaps Sir Isaac Newton was right and light is a particle after all.

What Color Is Light?

But perhaps James Maxwell was right. Light comes in tiny waves. Some waves are short; some are long. When we see *colors*, we are seeing light of different wavelengths. Even though sunlight (or what scientists call *white light*) appears to be colorless, it is actually a mixture of many colors or wavelengths of light. Check out the sky after a rain and you can see some of these colors as a rainbow. As sunlight is reflected through raindrops, it is bent. Light with long wavelengths, like red, is bent more than light with short wavelengths, like violet. You can separate sunlight into a rainbow or *spectrum* much like the famous scientist Sir Isaac Newton did some 300 years ago.

What You Need:

- A straight-sided, clear, glass tumbler.
- A piece of card with a 2-inch-long (5 cm) vertical slit.
- A sheet of white paper.
- Adhesive tape.
- A window ledge or table beside the window.

What You Need To Do:

Fill the glass with water and tape the card on so that the slit is against one side of the glass. Place the white paper close to a window, on a wide ledge or table, and stand the glass on it. Make sure the card with the slit is facing the window.

What Do You See?

Sunlight passing through the slit is bent by the water in the glass. This gives you the awesome spectrum on the paper. Just like the rainbow in the sky, the water bends the white light pouring in the window into the fan of colors that you see. (To remember the order of the colors try remembering the name Roy G Biv, which stands for red, orange, yellow, green, blue, indigo, and violet.)

Check This Out:

If you have a prism at home, try using it in place of the glass of water.

If you can get hold of two prisms (or try experimenting with a second glass of water), you should be able to make the colored light rays combine again to form white light.

Toolbox: Observation

"Excuse me, Dr. Lenslo. Did I just see you talking to your pencil?" asked Dr. Paige.

"Shhhhh. I'm on the air," Dr. Lenslo whispered.

"On the air?"

"I'll explain during the next commercial. You just keep playing with those black balls of yours."

"Sometimes I think you're catching too much light."

"For your information, wordy one, I'm practicing the scientific process of observation," Dr. Lenslo responded indignantly.

"And the pencil?" Dr. Paige inquired.

"What I was observing."

"Since when does observing involve talking to a pencil?"

"You really ought to dust off your pages sometime. Okay, I'll explain. I was pretending to be a DJ, and my radio audience just happens to love hearing about pencils. It's their hobby. Anyway, as you may know, DJs must have the gift of gab . . . they can't stop talking because not talking is what they call *dead air*."

"I still don't see what all of this has to do with observation," Dr. Paige stated.

"Well, how do you keep talking about something if you aren't really good at observing that thing? I was in training, you see?"

"Fascinating. Now that your training is over, why not see how good you are at really observing."

"What did you have in mind?" Dr. Lenslo asked.

"You see these black balls? I want you to tell me which one weighs the most simply by observing them."

"For me, expert scientist that I am, that's no problem. I observe that the biggest one is most likely the most massive."

"Are you observing or guessing?"

"Observing."

"I'm afraid not, expert scientist. Observing involves all the senses, not just your eyes. Had you really been observing, you would have reached out and held the balls in your hands. Very quickly you would have come to the conclusion that the biggest ball is not the heaviest. The smallest is."

"Wow. That's pretty neat. You used another sense: touch. You get my certificate for *Observer of the Year!*"

Catch a Wave

Ready for a trip to the beach? Sorry, not this time. The waves I'm talking about have nothing to do with water. They're *electromagnetic waves* . . . the kind that make up the rainbow of colors you've just seen. Of course, without them you wouldn't be able to see the beach. There are other types of invisible electromagnetic waves on either side of the rainbow-colored light: radio waves, microwaves, ultraviolet waves, X-rays, and infrared waves.

These electromagnetic waves have different wavelengths which determine their energy and function. You wouldn't want to wear stereo headphones, for example, that were giving off X-rays. Or use radio waves to bake a cake.

Want to keep an electromagnetic wave from having an effect? Find something to block it. A lead blanket, for example, blocks X-rays. Your eyelids block most visible light. What does it take to block infrared (IR) rays?

It just so happens that your TV remote control works by sending infrared rays to a sensor on your TV or VCR. You can experiment with it next time your dad is channel surfing.

IR Blockers

What You Need:
• A TV or VCR with wireless remote control.
• A tape measure.
• A variety of "test" IR blockers: paper, plastic, wood, etc.

What You Need To Do:
Find the maximum distance from which your remote control will operate your TV or VCR. Start near the set and slowly move back, testing to see if the remote works every, say, 10 inches (25 cm). Aim the remote directly at the set.

When you've found the maximum distance from which the remote works, measure and record it.

Now place what you think might be a good IR "blocker" in front of the remote, between it and the TV. Try paper, plastic, your brother . . . Does the remote still work to the maximum distance? Does the material weaken the signal so it only works at closer distances? Or does the material totally block the signal?

Repeat this for all test materials. Which materials worked as blockers? Which didn't?

Something To Think About:
Do the same materials that block IR block visible light? Design an experiment and find out. Could TV remote controls use visible light? Why or why not?

TV Like Never Before

Watching TV wouldn't be nearly as much fun if you couldn't see it. Want to watch it like you never have before? No, this isn't an invitation to park in front of it and be a sponge. There are better things to be doing with your brain than letting it soak up too much TV. The fact is, this is a case of watching TV without even turning it on. Want to give it a try?

What You Need:

- Your color television from the last activity. The TV should be plugged in.
- A good flashlight.
- A dark room.
- Your hand.

What You Need To Do:

Make sure the room is very dark. Place your hand on the TV screen and hold it very still. Shine the flashlight on the TV screen. Move the light around so every part of the TV screen, except for the part covered by your hand, gets the flashlight shining on it. Turn off the flashlight and remove your hand.

What Do You See?

You should see a dark image of your hand on a glowing TV screen. Now that's watching TV! There are little particles in the TV tube that get excited by light. It makes them glow. That's why you get a light-picture when you watch television. The flashlight is a weak light, so it gives these particles a weak charge, just strong enough for you to see the area covered by your hand. Those particles were not excited and didn't glow.

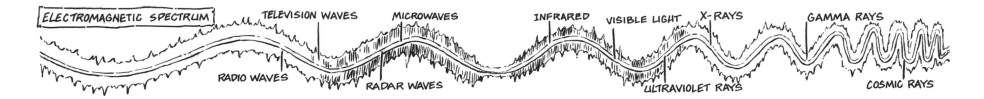

ELECTROMAGNETIC SPECTRUM — TELEVISION WAVES — MICROWAVES — INFRARED — VISIBLE LIGHT — X-RAYS — GAMMA RAYS — RADIO WAVES — RADAR WAVES — ULTRAVIOLET RAYS — COSMIC RAYS

Archimedes' Death Ray

Once upon a time, in about 214 B.C. to be more precise, the Greek scientist Archimedes supposedly saved his hometown by using the awesome power of light. Light not only allows you to experience a world of color, it also allows you to get things done. Light is a form of *energy* . . . you can do work with it . . . or even save your hometown from invading Roman soldiers. To get a feel for this energy, try this experiment.

What You Need:
• A magnifying lens.
• A mirror.
• Some small scraps of paper and wood.
• An outdoor spot like a cement sidewalk or driveway that doesn't have a lot of things that could burn easily . . . you don't want things like dry grass around.

What You Need To Do:
On a sunny day take your materials outside and practice focusing the light of the sun onto the paper. Use the magnifying lens or mirror. Try to focus the light into as small a spot as you can. Notice that as the point of light on the paper gets smaller it also gets brighter . . . and hotter. Ouch!

Of course, being a good scientist, you ask yourself how this happens. With this experiment, you might be able to make a good argument for light being a particle. Think of a particle of sand that some playful friend tosses your way at the beach. One particle you would hardly notice. On the other hand, a handful of particles that suddenly splatted on your back just might get your attention. Focusing means to take everything (all the particles) and bring them together at a point. Light is energy. It's moving (at 186,000 miles per second). The more particles of light you have hitting your paper, the more energy (in the form of heat) you're going to feel.

If you have some time on your hands, you might even burn your initials, or a design or picture, into a piece of scrap wood (not your parents' sundeck). Be creative.

Like the artist who fashioned a universe, you have been made to be creative. Creativity and art are one type of worship. Ever heard of Michelangelo? Now there was an artist! Michelangelo spent over 3 years painting the famous Sistine Chapel so that it retells the Genesis story of creation. See what you can come up with on your piece of wood. I'll check on you in 3 years.

To finish the story . . . Archimedes had his soldiers focus the sunlight from many small mirrors onto the ships of the advancing Roman fleet. The ships burned before they could make it to shore. Light saves a city!

Archimedes' creative defense of his town was reenacted in 1973 when soldiers holding 70 mirrors focused the light of the sun onto an empty row boat about 160 feet off shore. Poof! No more row boat. Archimedes' idea really worked!

What Do You See?

Lasers (Light Amplification by Stimulated Emission of Radiation) are another application of the power of light. Unlike the light that comes from a plain old light bulb, laser light is all traveling in the same direction at the same speed. Think of it as millions of soldiers all marching to the beat of the same drum.

Lasers have so much light packed into such a small space (much like you had when you focused the sunlight through your magnifying lens or mirror onto the paper) that surgeons can use them to make delicate cuts. The heat from the beam seals blood vessels as it cuts, making operations almost bloodless. Manufacturers use laser beams for cutting and welding metal. A number of everyday tasks are also accomplished by lasers. Visit your local supermarket and notice the laser light that scans groceries for price codes at the checkout counter.

Light from Unexpected Sources

This experiment must be done in total darkness. Try a closet at night, using a towel to block out any light that might shine under the bottom of the door.

What You Need:
- Newspapers to lay on the floor to catch any mess.
- Several wintergreen hard candies. Broken ones are fine. The ones with a hole in the center work best.
- A good pair of pliers.

What You Need To Do:
Place one candy piece in the jaws of the pliers. Be sure that you're in total darkness. Hold the pliers close enough

to see and carefully squeeze them as hard as possible. You may have to use both hands to apply enough pressure.

What Do You See?
There will be a brief, faint glow of light very near the candy. You may have to try several times for a good result. Pressure is the key. As a bit of an explanation, consider what the candy is made of: sugar. Sugar is an energy food. Your body keeps a storehouse of a type of sugar (glycogen) in your liver always ready for when you get out of bed in the morning. Run a mile and you really begin to use that energy. Some of that energy in sugar can be *converted to light energy*. Interesting.

Check This Out:
Some people have even reported flashes of light from simply stirring a glass bowl of granulated white sugar! Try it.

Speaking of light from unexpected sources, consider the firefly. Here's an insect that can produce its own light without producing heat. That's a whole lot more efficient than any light bulb ever designed by people! The eerie cold light the firefly produces is *chemical light* very similar to the light produced in these experiments.

Trivia

In Brazil, fireflies have been caged in hollow vessels and used as lanterns. Some young people even tie them in their hair or to their ankles when walking at night! The brightest fireflies give off enough light to read by.

A Challenge

You're welcome to prove me wrong, but I say you can't see a penny through a glass of water. Want to take the challenge?

What You Need:
- A plain clear glass (or disposable clear plastic cup) filled with water.
- A penny.
- A saucer or small piece of paper.

What You Need To Do:
Place the glass of water on top of the penny and cover the top of the glass with the saucer or paper.

What Do You See?
Don't strain your eyes. You won't see the penny. Recall how we said light rays are bent by going through things like water? This is such a situation. The only way you can see the penny is by looking straight down, and the saucer prevents you from doing that.

Check This Out:
For another strange illusion, take the saucer away and look at the surface of the water from the side. The penny seems to be on top of the water!

This bending of light is called *refraction*. A simpler example can be seen by placing a pencil in a half-full clear glass of water. When you stand back and look, the pencil seems broken. Why? Well, the only reason you see the pencil at all is because light bounces off it into your eyes. But light is coming from two places: the pencil in the water and the pencil outside the water. There's no problem with the light coming from the pencil outside the water. As expected, it follows the rules and travels in a straight line. But the light coming from the pencil (and penny) in the water follows another rule as it passes through the water to the air on its way to your eyes: the rule of refraction. When the light hits the tiny molecules making up the water and glass, it bounces and changes direction just a bit: It's refracted.

Among other things, refraction explains why a fish looks bigger under water and why objects can appear to be 3 feet deep when they are really 4. Refraction also gives you a good reason never to dive into a pool without knowing its actual depth.

Parting Shot

"Light, like everything else God made, follows rules," Dr. Paige declared. "Have you ever played a sport like basketball? Imagine if no one bothered to learn the rules. One team might decide to play with two balls, 16 players, and all the traveling they wanted. The other team might decide their best strategy is to put a trampoline under their net for easier dunkings. Not a chance! Things always work better if someone who understands the game makes up some rules."

"Makes sense," Dr. Lenslo admitted.

"Did you know, for example," Dr. Paige continued excitedly, "that light always travels in a straight line unless it hits something or is pulled on by gravity? (We'll learn more about gravity in Day 4.) Try shining a flashlight around a corner to check it out . . . It's a rule, and you can count on it. In fact, if you wake up late at night and find yourself in darkness it sure is comforting to know that, when you flip that light switch, light is going to follow the rule!"

"Okay, Dr. Paige, I'm impressed. Never again will I think of light as that wimpy 40 watter hangin' in my closet," Dr. Lenslo declared. "I do have a question, however."

"Thought you might."

"Well, seems to me that all these rules about light, like the one about always traveling in straight lines, suggest that someone must have made the rule book. I've played a bit of basketball in my day, and I know that rule books don't make themselves. So let's clear this up. Who made the rules? Scientists?"

"Charming question, Dr. Lenslo. Did you know that some of my best pals are rule books? I suspect this is one of those questions, however, that you already know the answer to. Allow me to respond. Scientists study light and a great many other things. They notice that light always behaves in certain ways. They describe this behavior and may, in fact, give it a name. Under no circumstances, good friend, do the scientists create this behavior. The scientist only describes the design that the designer has fashioned."

"Nicely said. I know the designer: God! God made the rules and wrote the rule book. I like it."

DAY 2

GOD MADE AIR AND WATER

Genesis 1:6–8: *Then God said, "Let there be something to divide the water in two!" So God made the air. . . . Some of the water was above the air, and some of the water was below it. God named the air "sky." Evening passed, and morning came. This was the second day.* (ICB)

Once you were a baby. Trust me. You were pillow-soft, sweet, and ever so fragile. Someone who loved you dearly wrapped you in the warmest blanket they could find and snuggled you close in their protective arms. You were rocked gently to sleep, peacefully unaware you were in the safest place you could be.

The world you live in is similarly wrapped in a thick blanket of gases, called the *atmosphere*. Without this blanket to protect us, we would be roasted by the sun during the day, then frozen at night as all its heat escaped into space. You've probably forgotten about your baby blanket, and you're forgiven if you've never really appreciated the blanket of air around our planet. After all, the atmosphere is colorless, odorless, and tasteless. It's very easy to forget it's there. Keep in mind, however, that you could not live without it and, like your baby blanket, it didn't just happen to wrap itself around you. God made the blanket.

Air under Water

Ahh! Nothing like a breath of fresh *air*! Take in a big, deep one. Feel it all the way down to your big toe. Great stuff. To really appreciate air, you might try going without for a while. Nothing permanent here. Simply try holding your breath for one minute. Don't let any of that precious air reach your lungs. Not a lovely experience. Right? Air is the "stuff of life." If you don't like it, consider moving to the moon. (See Day 4.)

Air is a form of matter. Like all other matter, air takes up space (or has *volume*) and weighs something (or has *mass*). Want to prove it?

Pouring Air

What You Need:
- 2 transparent plastic cups.
- A large transparent container. (A small aquarium, without the fish, would be perfect, but your bathtub would work as well.)

What You Need To Do:
Fill the large container with about 8 inches of water. Hold one cup in each hand upside down and push them under water. Fill one of the cups with water by holding it slanted. Don't

leave any bubbles of air. Now we have one cup filled with water in the one hand, and one cup with air in the other (still under water).

Now push the cup with air a little lower than the other cup and pour the air into the water-filled cup by slowly slanting the air-filled cup. Catch the bubbles of air in your other cup.

If you like, try repeating this back and forth from one cup to the other.

What Do You See?

Hopefully you saw that air takes up space. You started with what looked like 2 empty cups. Fact is, those cups were full of air. Now, think about it. If something is full, can you add anything else? No way. Until you slanted one of the cups and allowed the lighter-than-water air to escape, no water could enter the cup.

Keeping Paper Dry under Water

Have you ever wondered how people work under water to build the foundations of a bridge? How do you breathe at the bottom of a river? How do you stay dry? Good questions. You're getting the hang of this scientist thing. Now for the answers.

Just pretend that you are a piece of paper.

What You Need:
- A dry transparent plastic cup.
- A large transparent container (large enough to fit your hand in).
- A dry piece of paper. (No, don't tear one out of this book. Get one that no one minds getting wrinkled.)

What You Need To Do:

Fill the large container about ¾ full with water. Crumple a piece of dry paper and squeeze it into the bottom of the plastic cup. Turn the cup upside down (making sure that the crumpled paper stays up in the cup) and push it completely under the water. Keep the cup vertical. Hang out there for a while if you want, but stay vertical.

Now back the cup out of the water and let the water drip off. Do not shake it off. Take the crumpled paper out of the cup with a dry hand and check to see if it stayed dry.

What Do You See?

The paper is dry! Air *takes up space*. Besides the crumpled paper, there was air in the cup that would not allow water to enter. So, now you know how to stay dry under water. Put a large water-tight container on the bottom of the river and pump in air . . . no need to worry about water rushing in, since the container is already full of air.

Trivia
On an average day your lungs move enough air in and out to fill a medium-sized room or blow up several thousand party balloons.

Heavy Air

Since air is matter, it not only has volume, but *mass* as well. Air weighs something. That's right, your basketball that is pumped to perfection actually weighs more than when it's flat. Of course, to actually measure this, and measuring is marvellous, you would need a rather accurate scale. If you don't have access to one, consider this experiment.

What You Need:
- 2 straws.
- A pin.
- 2 identical pieces of transparent adhesive tape.
- 2 identical uninflated balloons.
- A pen.

What You Need To Do:
Balance a straw on your finger so that it's perfectly horizontal. Push a pin through the straw where it's balancing and attach it to the end of the other straw. This second straw will be your handle. You have just built a balance.

Make 2 small loops (sticky side out) of the transparent tape. Attach one loop of tape to one end of the balance and the other loop to the other end. Adjust the tape so that everything remains balanced. Now attach the balloons to the sticky tape. If the balloons are the same, everything should balance. Adjust, if necessary.

Take one balloon off. Blow it up and then re-attach it to your balance.

What Do You See?
The balloons no longer balance each other. The balloon with air weighs more than the uninflated balloon and pulls down that side of the balance.

Check This Out:
Have a lung-air contest with a friend. Each of you take an identical balloon and blow it up with one big breath. Or, if you want, two breaths. The important thing is for you each to blow the same way into your own balloon. Now attach the balloons to your straw balance from the previous experiment. Who blows more hot air? Whose lungs weigh more?

Want more dramatic proof that air is heavy? Try the next experiment.

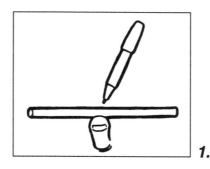
2.

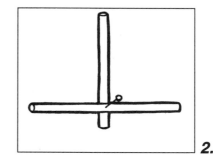
1.

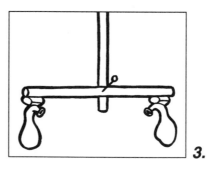
3.

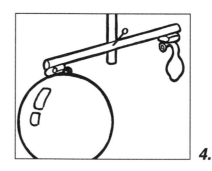
4.

Trivia
All of the folds of the lungs result in a surface area 40 times larger than the skin's area and large enough to carpet a small apartment.

Karate Kid

What You Need:
- 1 or 2 sheets of newspaper.
- A stick of pine (roughly ¼ x 1 x 30 inches). An old ruler will work.

What You Need To Do:
Lay the stick on a smooth table so it hangs over the edge 6 inches (15 cm). (What would happen if you hit the end of the stick hanging over the edge? Go ahead. Try it. Now replace the stick.) Cover the stick with newspaper, right to the edge of the table. With your left hand, smooth down the paper. Strike the end of the stick a sudden sharp blow with the edge of your hand.

What Do You See?
The stick breaks! The blanket of air that is our atmosphere is heavy. It has *pressure*. You can feel it on your face when you walk into the wind or ride your bike. It's this pressure that broke the stick. When you smoothed the paper down, you made sure there was almost no air under it. But a whole atmosphere exists above the paper and pushes down on it. Scientific types use numbers to describe forces. There is about 15 pounds per square inch pushing down on the paper. Measure the area of the newspaper you used (length x width) in inches and then calculate the total force of the atmosphere pushing on it. For example, the force pushing down on a 20 x 40-inch piece of newspaper is 20 x 40 x 15 pounds = 12,000 pounds; that's more than a minivan. No wonder it was impossible to lift with a thin stick!

"Ouch! All this air pressure pushing down on us! Why aren't we crushed, Dr. Paige?"

"Flattened out a little, you'd make a fine bookmark, Dr. Lenslo. But not to worry, air pressure not only pushes down, it pushes in all directions. Say a friend pushes you. What happens?"

"I fall over."

"But if another friend pushes from the other direction at the same time you won't fall. The pressures balance each other."

"I'm thrilled to hear it."

"You aren't crushed because God designed an atmosphere that pushes from all directions equally at the same time. You're safe."

All about Nothing

When there is a space with no air, we call it a *vacuum*. This word comes from another word that means "empty." We all know that some things that look empty aren't necessarily so. You might decide to clean your room (your mother would appreciate this) by emptying it. Out go the socks from under the bed, the cat from on the bed, and the bed itself. You spend the afternoon emptying your room. But is it really empty? Of course not. What you have left in your room is wall-to-wall air.

You knew that. What you may not have known is that that wall-to-wall air is made up of molecules. Molecules are the really tiny pieces of stuff that everything is made of. You, me, chocolate shakes, and air are all made of molecules. Now, molecules are bouncing around, like kernels in a popcorn popper—always moving and vibrating. When air molecules bump into things they make air pressure.

A vacuum, on the other hand, is really empty. Empty of everything, including air molecules. And when there are no air molecules, there's no air pressure.

Check It Out:

Try tying a string to a slightly moist suction cup. Press the cup to the top of a smooth-topped stool. Lift the string. Amazing. You can pick up the stool with just the suction cup. All because you pushed the air out of the cup to

create a vacuum. Of course, the pressure of the air molecules outside the cup remains the same and pushes the cup firmly down on the stool.

The Magdeburg Spheres

This experiment took place in 1664 before Emperor Ferdinand III. Two metal hemispheres were fitted together. (A hemisphere is half a sphere, like a ball cut in half across the middle.) Then a vacuum pump sucked all the air out. It took 16 horses to pull the hemispheres apart!

Try it. Take 2 heavy rubber plungers (used to unplug sinks). Get a friend to help you push the 2 plungers together. Now try to pull them apart.

Need a few extra horsepower?

The Straw Drinking Race

What You Need:
• 2 identical drinking straws (one punctured with 7 to 10 needle holes over the whole length).
• 2 small cups half filled with something you like to drink.

What You Need To Do:
Challenge a friend to a race. If you intend to win, hand your friend the straw with the holes in it. First one to empty his or her cup wins.

What Do You See?
You win. But being the kind person you are, you explain that being a good sucker requires the ability to create a vacuum. When you sucked on your straw, you sucked most of the air molecules out of the straw and into your mouth. This made a vacuum in the straw. Then the air pressure in the room pushed down on the top of the drink and pushed it up through your straw. Right into your mouth. Mmmmm.

The Old Upside-Down-Glass-of-Water Trick

What You Need:
• A clear plastic cup.
• Some water.
• A postcard.

What You Need To Do:
Fill the cup to the top with water. Take the postcard, wet it slightly, and put it on the top of the cup. Holding the postcard against the cup, turn the whole thing upside down. Carefully remove your hand from the postcard.

What Do You See?
You'll see a space inside the cup . . . between the bottom of the cup and the top of the water. That space is another vacuum . . . no air, no air pressure. But there's lots of air in the room outside the cup. The pressure of the air in the room pushes up against the postcard so it sticks to the cup and holds the water inside. No magic here; just science.

Check It Out:
Try it with larger containers and larger cards. How big can the container be and the air pressure still be greater than the weight of the water pushing down on the card?

What's in Air?

Good question. One thing we know for sure is that air is a *gas*. In fact, air is a mixture of gases. More than ¾ of the atmosphere (78%) is made up of the gas nitrogen, and most of the rest (21%) is oxygen. It is the gas oxygen that you need to breathe. Oxygen is also the gas that flames need to burn. This leaves about 1% that is carbon dioxide, water vapor, and a bunch of other gases. The water vapor portion of air is easy to demonstrate by putting a clear glass in the freezer for a few minutes and then breathing on it when you take it out. The cloudiness that forms on the cold glass is the result of warm moist air from your lungs turning back into liquid water on the cold surface. We call this *condensation*. As for *oxygen* . . .

What You Need:
- A candle.
- A large glass jar taller than the candle.
- An egg cup.
- A cake pan.
- Water.
- Matches . . . and adult supervision.

What You Need To Do:
Stick the candle to the egg cup with a bit of melted wax and place it in the middle of the cake pan. Fill the cake pan about ¾ full of water, making sure the candle is well clear of the surface of the water. Light the candle and leave it to burn for a couple of minutes. Place the jar over the candle. You'll have to tilt it, at first, to let some air out and some water in. (Remember? Air takes up space.) You want the water levels in the jar and pan to be the same.

What Do You See?
The candle will go out as soon as all of the oxygen is used up. The water level will rise in the jar by about a fifth to take the place of the oxygen that has been used up. Conclusion? Air must contain about a fifth of its volume in oxygen.

What about carbon dioxide? Check out the next page.

Carbon Dioxide

Just like oxygen and the other gases that make up our atmosphere, *carbon dioxide* has its own particular properties. The bubbles in soft drinks and the fog special-effects on TV and movies are two pleasant results of these properties. Less pleasant is the fact that carbon dioxide is the gas responsible for what you may have heard called the "greenhouse effect."

Just like glass in a greenhouse, carbon dioxide traps heat from the sun and keeps it from escaping into space. Without carbon dioxide our cozy blanket of an atmosphere wouldn't be nearly as comfortable. What about having too much carbon dioxide? Every time we burn something in the air—gas in our cars, oil in our homes, wood in our fireplaces—we increase the amount of carbon dioxide in the air and increase the greenhouse effect.

It's interesting that the same gas produced by burning may also be used to put out fires.

What You Need:
- Baking soda.
- Vinegar.
- A glass bottle, such as a small soft-drink bottle.
- A saucer.
- A candle.
- A tablespoon measure.
- Non-hardening modeling clay (see our recipe on page 155).
- Matches.
- Adult supervision.

What You Need To Do:
Stick the candle to the saucer with a bit of the modeling clay. Put the candle on a table well away from anything that could catch fire. Light the candle. Put 1 tablespoon of baking soda into the bottle (you may wish to roll up a piece of paper to use as a funnel—much less of a mess to clean up afterward). Pour about 3 tablespoons of vinegar into the bottle. When the vinegar touches the soda, they react to form the invisible gas carbon dioxide. Carefully "pour" the carbon dioxide gas over the flame, taking care not to burn your fingers or let any of the liquid escape from the bottle.

What Do You See?
Carbon dioxide gas is heavier than air, so it won't float out of the bottle but will sit on top of the vinegar solution. When you tip the bottle, the invisible fumes of carbon dioxide will "pour" out and put out the candle flame immediately.

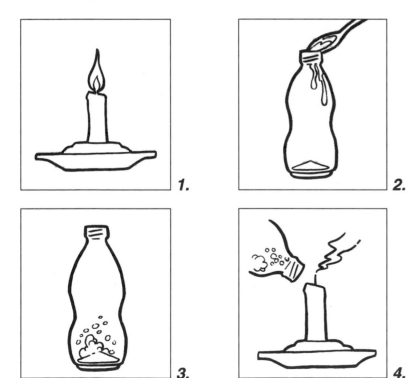

1.

2.

3.

4.

Toolbox: Evidence

"If you could spare a moment from brushing your teeth, Dr. Lenslo . . ." Dr. Paige asked, hopefully.

"You have something against brushing teeth?"

"Not really, but 26 times a day?"

"Evidence, Dr. Paige. I'm gathering evidence."

"I'll give you evidence, Lenslo. This skull I've been examining is full of it."

"I'd be happy to bury the thing if you like."

"No thanks. I do appreciate the way you like to look for evidence by doing science, rather than just reading about it, Dr. Lenslo. But sometimes experimenting isn't possible. Let's say you believe kids who visit Venus for 6 months of the year will have fewer cavities. How could you prove such a thing? No, sometimes we must make decisions based, not only on what we do, but on what we read in books, watch on television, or hear from teachers."

"You want me to brush the skull's teeth?"

"Not yet. Dr. Lenslo, meet Kittywampus. According to Wister's dictionary, Kittywampus is 'an ill-adapted nocturnal animal that became extinct during the last Ice Age.'"

"So, he's an animal that hunted at night long ago. Nice teeth," Dr. Lenslo added admiringly. "Ooh, great pointy canines!"

"Carnivore. Kittywampus was a meat eater. But that's not all this skull can tell us. Notice that one side of his skull is a mirror image of the other? *Bilateral symmetry*."

"Hey! I'm bilaterally symmetrical. My eye on one side is paired with my eye on the other. My arm on one side . . ."

"Fine, Dr. Lenslo. Now, take a peek inside. See all the empty space? That's his cranial capacity, the space that held his brain. Pretty good size, eh? More evidence that Kittywampus must have shown moves and smarts similar to animals with this size brain."

"What's this hole at the back tell you, Dr. Paige?"

"I'm so glad you asked. That hole is the *foramen oval* (Latin for 'big hole'). It means Kittywampus ran around on all fours."

"Evidence?"

"Simple. The foramen oval is the opening through which the spinal cord enters the brain. If it's at the base of the skull, you're talking about an animal that walks upright. If it's at the back of the skull, the animal has to move on all fours. Kittywampus was a quadruped. Make sense?"

"Yes, indeed," Dr. Lenslo nodded.

"And there's more!" Dr. Paige exclaimed enthusiastically. "The flattened nose and forehead suggest Kittywampus appeared similar to a cat. As such, you might expect him to have a higher ratio of rod cells to cone cells in the retina of his eyes. After all, you can't hunt at night if you can't see your dinner."

"Anything else? I've got to go brush my teeth."

"Of course, there's more! Kittywampus was a mammal, gave birth to litters of . . . Forget it! Tell me. Why the tooth brushing?"

"Like I said, I'm looking for evidence. You know that commercial: 'Brush your teeth with Blest, you'll have cavities the less, and a smile forever fresh'? Well, they've got nerve suggesting doctors and scientists like ourselves recommend their toothpaste. I mean, what kind of evidence do they have?"

"None?"

"Precisely. What if one kid is two and another is twelve years old? What if one has a steady diet of sugar and has never gone to a dentist? I'm afraid I simply have to test the evidence myself."

"It would seem, Dr. Lenslo, that getting at the truth is important whether you're watching TV or simply listening to someone describe an old skull. Now, shall we ask our young scientist friends how good they are at examining the evidence? Hey, you! Yes, you, Reader. Find a piece of paper and jot down 10 facts about Kittywampus. Be careful. Examine your evidence."

"When you're finished," Dr. Lenslo added helpfully, "turn to page 153 and check your answer."

Reaching for the Sky

Reach for the sky. Stretch. Jump for it. If you keep eating your breakfast every morning and manage to grow to a height of 9 miles (not at all likely even with the best of breakfast cereals) you'll just be able to tickle the second layer of the atmosphere. The sky is like one of those less-than-healthy ice-cream sundaes stacked 5 layers thick. You live in the first layer (called the troposphere), which contains water vapor and enough air for us to breathe. Even at the top of the first layer, air gets very thin . . . which is why climbers on very tall mountains like Mt. Everest need to take air with them.

You were created to live in the *troposphere*, God's warm protective blanket. The troposphere is the perfect place for you to live. It has the right air, air pressure, temperature, and everything. The higher you go, things change. Have you ever wondered what it might be like a little higher up? We're not talking the top layers here. Unless you've signed up for the space shuttle, you're not going to be reaching the ionosphere (up to 310 miles). No, let's be content with being a high-flying bird, a helicopter, or even a weather balloon. That's it. A weather balloon.

What You Need:

- A helium balloon. The biggest one you can lay your hands on.
- A fishing rod and reel.
- A small thermometer.
- Strong thread.

What You Need To Do:

Tie both the helium balloon and the thermometer to the end of your fishing line. Be careful not to let any sharp objects near your balloon. Record the temperature and then "go fishing" well away from trees and electrical wires. Release the balloon and let it slowly pull your line toward the sky. After about 20 minutes, reel in your balloon and check the temperature.

What Do You See?

Your thermometer tells you it's colder up there. How much colder is going to depend on things like how high your balloon could pull the line and how much wind is blowing.

Check It Out:

Try your weather balloon on days with different types of weather and see what difference it makes. Are windy days colder? (Do **not** try this experiment on stormy days when lightning is present as some fishing rods contain metal parts.)

Temperature isn't the only thing that changes as you go higher in the atmosphere. Air pressure changes as well. This fact can make life uncomfortable for someone who climbs mountains. When the kettle boils for soup or tea on a mountain, the water will only be lukewarm. On high mountains you won't be able to cook an egg or rice even if the water is boiling. Boiling, you see, doesn't mean "hot." Boiling is simply the name scientists give to the rapid change of something from liquid form to gas. And air pressure affects this just as much as temperature.

In fact, believe it or not, if it wasn't for air pressure pushing on all the tiny molecules of water in our lakes and oceans, they would be boiling all the time! (Good thing God planned it out right, isn't it?)

As you get higher and higher on a mountain, the weight of the atmosphere above you becomes less and less. Why? Because some of the troposphere is now below you. This means there is less air pressure pushing on the water molecules to keep them as water molecules. If the pressure is reduced enough, the molecules escape the liquid to become a gas. That's what boiling is. Fascinating!

Check It Out:

If you know an adult (a science teacher, maybe) who has a vacuum pump, ask him or her to suck all the air molecules out of a container with half a cup of water in it. The water boils . . . at room temperature! Try other materials—marshmallows, for example.

Rain, Rain, Go Away

Knowing that it gets colder the higher up you go gives you part of an explanation for how the water on our Earth gets recycled. To learn more, try making some *rain*.

What You Need
- 2 shallow trays or regular dinner plates.
- A water kettle.
- Water and ice.
- Oven mitts.
- Adult supervision.

What You Need To Do:
Heat water in the kettle until it's boiling. (Watch out for the steam—it's a lot hotter than the boiling water.) With your oven mitts safely on, hold a tray or upside-down plate in the steam that comes from the kettle. Put a few ice cubes on the first plate. Place the second plate under the first one to catch the drops of rain. Pour the water from the second plate back into the kettle to complete the *water cycle*.

What Do You See?
Thanks for the rain. Your kettle can be compared to the ocean water being heated by the sun. As the ocean water turns to a gas (steam in this case), it rises higher and higher into the colder atmosphere. Your ice cubes act like the cold, high atmosphere. Along the way clouds form, and you know what happens next. As molecules of moist air get colder, they begin to slow down. When they slow down enough, they begin to stick to each other. If enough of them stick together, they get too heavy to be supported by the air pressure. That's what raindrops are . . . wee molecules that hang on to each other until they become too heavy and fall on you as rain.

This is the kind of knowledge people use to predict the weather. However, even with the best of equipment, forecasting the weather is an inexact science. Like light, the atmosphere follows rules. But only God knows them all. Next time you need a real weather forecast, check with him.

Trivia
At Browning, Montana, during a single 24-hour period, the temperature fell 100 degrees Fahrenheit—from 44°F to -56°F! For the highest temperatures recorded on Earth you need to visit the Sahara desert. At Al Azizyan, the hottest shade temperature was recorded on September 13, 1922—136.4°F.

A Cloud in a Bottle

So *clouds* are due to cold and pressure. Not sure you believe us? Want to see pressure at work before your very eyes? You don't have to climb a high mountain for this one.

What You Need:
• A large clear plastic soft-drink bottle (torpedo shaped).
• Warm water.
• A match.
• Adult supervision.

What You Need To Do:
Pour enough warm water into the bottle to just cover the bottom. Hold the bottle horizontally. Light the match, blow it out, and then quickly hold the smoking match near the mouth of the bottle. Slowly squeeze the bottle, then release your pressure on it so a little smoke is sucked inside. Put the top on the bottle, tighten it, and swish the water around a few times. While holding the bottle up to a bright light, squeeze and release the bottle several times. Look closely in the center of the bottle.

What Do You See?
You should see a cloud form every time the bottle is released, then disappear when the bottle is squeezed.

When you lower the pressure inside the bottle by releasing it, the water vapor from the hot water condenses into a cloud. This is exactly like climbing a very high mountain and seeing the effects of reduced air pressure. Remember how easy it is to make water boil on a mountain? When you remove pressure from above a liquid, it's going to let molecules escape from the liquid into the air. And what's another name for liquid in the air? You got it. A cloud.

Of course, the opposite of this happens when you add pressure. The squeezed bottle increases the air pressure and forces the water molecules back into the liquid water. Bye, bye, cloud. So now you know. Not only does a drop in temperature affect weather, but so does a change in air pressure.

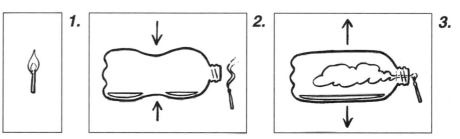

Parting Shot

"Why, Dr. Lenslo, if the Almighty chose to give you two legs, do you stand on one?"

"I'm balancing. And thinking. Ever tried walking along a narrow fence?"

"Well, yes," Dr. Paige recalled. "I was a gymnast in school . . . had to do a lot of balancing then."

"What happened when you lost your balance?"

"Nothing very nice, I'm afraid. Usually it meant a fall, bruises, pain . . . I don't like to think about it. What are you thinking, Dr. Lenslo?"

"I'm thinking balance is important."

"Indeed it is," agreed Dr. Paige. "Our atmosphere, for example, is in balance. Think what our planet would be like if . . ." Dr. Paige got excited, "God had chosen an atmosphere of only 1% oxygen."

"Gasp. The possibility leaves me breathless," Dr. Lenslo wheezed, almost losing his balance.

"God put just the right amounts of the gases into our atmosphere to support life." Dr. Paige spoke fast in her excitement. "And the correct gases, too. What if, instead of nitrogen, 78% of our atmosphere was the gas propane?" she asked suddenly.

"Goodness, me! Every time someone lit a match we'd all be barbecued," Dr. Lenslo fired back.

"God had a lot of choices. Instead of 78% of air being a gas like nitrogen, which we breathe safely, God might have designed the atmosphere of poisonous gases like hydrogen chloride! Smelly gases like hydrogen sulphide! Or gases like helium that would make us all sound like Donald Duck!"

"I'm just glad he gave us an atmosphere. I can't imagine living in a vacuum!"

"You can't imagine it, my balancing buddy, because you couldn't live in one," Dr. Paige suggested. "Life can only result from balance. Even our air pressure is perfect for life. Any more—we'd be crushed. Any less—we'd be vaporized. And think what effect it would have on the weather!"

"Blizzards in Arizona, and heat waves in Alaska."

Dr. Paige nodded. "Everything about our atmosphere . . . the gases making it up, the air pressure resulting from the gas molecules, and the weather, are in balance for a reason."

"I'd say that reason was life!" Dr. Lenslo stated with conviction.

"I'd say you're correct! You can stand on two feet again, Dr. Lenslo."

DAY 3

GOD MADE THE LAND, THE PLANTS, AND THE SEA

Genesis 1:9–13: *Then God said, "Let the water under the sky be gathered together so the dry land will appear." And it happened. God named the dry land "earth." He named the water . . . "seas." God saw that this was good.*
Then God said, "Let the earth produce plants. . . . Every seed will produce more of its own kind of plant." And it happened. . . . God saw that all this was good.
Evening passed, and morning came. This was the third day. (ICB)

Welcome to the planet Earth. Chances are you've never left it and, given the unfriendly conditions on all the other planets, you'll be wanting to stay for a while. Our Earth is an exciting place. There are mountains that soar so high their snow-covered peaks pierce the clouds, and there are valleys that are green and rich with growing plants. There is water everywhere. Rivers winding through marble canyons, vast oceans touching the shores of distant continents, lakes and streams and waterfalls. There are deserts, dry and threatening. Volcanoes, glaciers, caves, beaches, rocky cliffs . . . God has given us an endless variety of shapes and places to explore.

Exploring the Lord's Earth

As long as a hurricane isn't blowing, get the family together and go on a hike. Go somewhere you've never *explored* before . . . the mountains, the woods, the beach, or an inland lake shore. And do some science along the way!

Collect Stuff

Gather soil samples and label them with where they were found. Start a collection of rocks. Search for fossils. Collect and press leaves or wild flowers. If you don't have a plant press, you can place your beauties between 2 sheets of wax paper and pile all your encyclopedias on top. Get a plant identification book from your library and name and mount your specimens. Search for animal tracks, then photograph and identify them or make plaster casts of them. (Get an adult to help.) Collect samples of seeds and nuts.

Get alone. Really alone. Listen to the quiet. Talk to God. Better yet, wait and listen for him. Take time to enjoy the beauty around you. Smell the flowers, touch the tree bark, photograph the birds, eat a picnic lunch by a bubbling brook . . .

Scavenger Hunt

Get a few friends and go on a scavenger hunt. Use your imagination! Some of the things in our list can only be found with a good imagination. A famous scientist, Albert Einstein, once said, "Imagination is more important than knowledge." First one back with all of the items wins.

1. a square in nature
2. a seed
3. a candy wrapper
4. a broken egg shell
5. a circle in nature
6. evidence of animal life
7. a red C
8. a feather
9. an insect
10. evidence of man
11. a smooth rock
12. a hairy leaf
13. a tool
14. a piece of string
15. a piece of glass
16. something bumpy
17. something cool
18. something sculpted
19. something absorbent
20. something beautiful

Be Creative:

Finally, do something creative with what you experienced. You're the only living creature that can express your feelings in art. God expressed himself when he created. Who says scientists can't be artists? Write a poem. Draw or paint a picture. Compose a song. Awesome!

Dig It

Most people call it dirt, but *soil* is a better name. Where does it come from? Good question. One way soil forms is when rocks are broken down into bits smaller than sand. How? Try it.

What You Need:
- Rocks you've collected.
- Protective eye goggles.
- A sheet of newspaper to collect your soil.

What You Need To Do:
Hold a couple rocks over the piece of paper and rub them together. Push hard and grind off some rock dust. With your eye goggles on, put a rock on the paper and hit it with another. (Careful: Watch your fingers!) Try different pairs of rocks.

What Do You See?

Some rocks are harder than others. A piece of sandstone, for example, will scratch easily. On the other hand, to break granite it might take another piece of granite. It all depends on the *minerals* in the rock.

You probably noticed different shapes, sizes, and colors of rock dust. These are the result of the different minerals that make up your rocks. Tiny, clear pieces may be the mineral quartz. Milky white chunks could be the mineral calcite. All minerals (and there are a lot) have different properties, like hardness. Hardness is rated on a scale of 1 to 10, with 1 being the softest and 10 the hardest. The mineral talc (1) is so soft it's used to make baby powder. The mineral diamond (10) is so hard it will cut glass.

They don't say "hard as a rock" for nothing. At this rate it'll take you a few years to get enough soil to replant that favorite violet in your bedroom.

Water Power

The Earth weighs 5,974,000,000,000,000,000,000 tons, and a big part of its weight problem comes from soil. Obviously, most of the soil on Earth did not get here because God smashed some rocks together. God used and continues to use ocean waves, rushing water, windblown sand, and even sun and rain to *crumble rocks into soil*.

Which do you think is stronger? Water or rock? Or water or heavy cardboard? Be a good scientist and experiment to find out.

What You Need:
• One small empty milk carton.
• Water.
• A stapler.
• Adhesive tape.
• A freezer.

What You Need To Do:
Fill the empty milk carton all the way to the top with water, then staple across the top of the carton about 5 times. The top should be tightly shut. Tape over the top. Place the carton in the freezer. Leave it there until the water turns to ice . . . about 24 hours. What happens to the carton?

What Do You See?
Surprised? Thanks to water's wondrous talents, you will find that the carton has burst. Water is stronger! Good thing you didn't use a glass container.

Water can get into cracks in rocks. When the temperature drops below 32ºF, that water freezes into ice. Frozen water takes up more space than liquid water. So the water expands in the little cracks and breaks up the rocks. Quarter-inch iron balls that have been filled with water and then sealed have actually exploded violently when the water was suddenly frozen. This same power can very easily turn your rock into many tiny bits of rocks.

Water and ice are not the only way rock is changed to soil. You might visit quite a number of different national parks to see fascinating natural sculptures of rock that have been formed by the combination of wind and water.

Getting Dirty

Is soil just a bunch of broken rock? Check it out.

What You Need:

- Soil. Collect samples from your backyard, a vacant lot, the beach, a park, a swamp, and any other place you can collect soil. Label your containers.
- Water.
- Paper and pencil. Sometimes it's a really good idea to write down your observations. Imagine making a great discovery in science like a cure for cancer and then not being able to remember what you did!

What You Need To Do:

Pick up a handful of each of your soil samples. Look at them carefully. Rub a small amount of the soil between your fingers. How does it feel? Describe its texture. Write down your observations. Now add water to the containers of soil until each jar is ¾ full. Stir the soil and water together. Let the soil settle down in the water for at least ½ an hour. What are you observing? Anything floating on top of the water?

What Do You See?

You noticed that soil contains more than ground-up rocks. Scientists who study the earth (geologists) have fancy names for soil based on what they find in it. For example, if your soil sample contained lots of dead leaves and twigs as well as parts of bugs and other dead critters, they would say that it was a *humus* soil. Usually soils are made up of a mixture of humus plus ground-up rock of various sizes. When you added water to your containers of soils, it was the humus part that you saw floating on top. Other parts of the soil, clay for instance, would have turned the water cloudy but eventually settled to the bottom along with bits of gravel and sand.

Check This Out:

Besides being dirty, soil can be really interesting. You might want to design your own experiment using your soil collections. Which ones absorb the most water? Which ones allow you to grow things? Which ones would you build a house on? Interesting.

Cleaning Up

After all this messing around in the dirt, it's probably time for a bath. Would it surprise you to know:

- There is enough water in the world's oceans to fill 6,438,910,400,000,000,000 bathtubs?
- Over 70% of the surface of the Earth is covered with water?
- The Pacific Ocean alone covers a greater area than all the dry land on Earth put together?
- If the surface of the Earth were flat and all the water of the seas were evenly spread over it, it would be covered to a depth of 10 feet.

That's a lot of water!

Water is important for a great many reasons other than your need to bathe in it, skate on it, or brush your teeth with it. Remember the importance of the water cycle?

Obviously, your body needs water. You too are made up of more than 70% water and have to keep it that way by drinking a good amount of it each day. All this water is drawn from rivers, lakes, and wells and pumped through a maze of pipes to your faucet. Unless you have a taste for mud, you hope that what ends up in your drinking glass has been cleaned up a little.

Amazingly, much of the yuck of muddy water can be filtered out using good old soil. Find yourself a container, fill it with dirty water from a swamp or pond, and check for yourself.

What You Need:
- A cup of rinsed sand.
- A cup of washed gravel.
- A cup of coarsely broken, washed charcoal.
- A 6-inch (15 cm) clay flowerpot.
- A coffee filter.
- A large dish or shallow cake pan to collect your clean water in.
- A container with your dirty pond or swamp water in it.

What You Need To Do:
Make sure the clay pot is clean to start with. Line it with the filter paper and place it in the dish. Pack the pot with a layer of charcoal, then a layer of sand on top of the charcoal, then a layer of gravel. Gently pour a cup or two of your dirty pond water in a steady stream into your pot of soil. Wait for a couple minutes and see what comes out the bottom.

What Do You See?
If you compare the water you started out with with the water you ended up with, you'll notice that much of the yuck and guck that was in the pond water is missing. It ended up getting trapped or filtered by the soil and paper. What you have is cleaner water. It's cleaner, but not clean enough to drink.

In the water, invisible to you without a microscope, is an important ingredient that turns ground up rocks and dead plants into a soil that has got what it takes to grow your lunch. The missing part is the living part . . . germs.

A spoonful of good soil is said to contain more germs than there are people in this world. If you consider that it would take you a lot of spooning to fill an acre, you get a feel for the number of these living organisms. Germs aren't deserving of their nasty reputation . . . well, not in this case at least. If it were not for the germs in the soil, there wouldn't be the good stuff (nutrients) that get dissolved in water and made available to plants. When God designed the land, he designed it for life. He made sure all the parts needed to make life possible were ready and waiting.

Trivia

Just as your house is the place you call home, you are the place bacteria calls home. Close to 2,000 bacteria per square inch live on your legs, about 14,000 per square inch on your chest, and about 600,000 per square inch on your face!

Joke: How much soil may be removed from a hole that is 3 feet deep, 2 feet wide, and 10 feet long? Answer: None. There's no soil in a hole.

COFFEE FILTER

GRAVEL

SAND

CHARCOAL

Growing Lunch—the Plants

Life. Just what makes something alive? Observe something living. Something not living. What's the difference? Trees are living. Introduce yourself to one. Make friends with it. Give it a hug. Come on now, don't be shy. Sit back against your friendly green giant and dream about inventing the ultimate clean energy factory. Imagine a way to produce almost all the world's fuel, including its food, without polluting. Your factory's only waste product would be oxygen and water vapor. No smoke stacks, no oil spills, no rain forests chopped down, no streams and lakes damaged. As an added bonus, your factory would use up carbon dioxide, the "greenhouse" gas many scientists worry about.

An impossible dream? No way. You've already introduced yourself to such a factory. The fact is, any green plant is such a factory hard at work . . . a *photosynthesis factory*.

Inside a plant's leaves, in tiny jelly-bean shaped structures, you'll find the chief worker in the power plant . . . *chlorophyll*. This amazing chemical, famous for giving green plants their color ("chloro" is a Greek word meaning "green"), can actually trap light energy and work on it in assembly line fashion, converting it to sugar (glucose) and starch: food to feed themselves and every animal on Earth.

Green Test

What You Need:
- A healthy plant with broad leaves.
- A small piece of cardboard.
- A paper clip.
- A pair of scissors.

What You Need To Do:
Cut 2½-inch circles from the cardboard. Carefully, without disturbing the leaf, fix the circles to both sides of a leaf with the paper clip. After 4 days remove the circles.

What Do You See?
The area under the circles will be a visibly lighter color, perhaps even yellow. Chlorophyll, the green part of the leaf, is used to produce food for the plant. Without sunlight, the chlorophyll can't produce food to sustain itself and the plant. Chlorophyll in the rest of the leaf keeps producing food and remains green.

You get hold of the products of these fabulous factories every time you bite into an apple or chew on a burger. (Remember, that burger got its energy when it was a cow eating photosynthetic grass.) You also tap into it every time your family burns wood or fossil fuels like coal and oil. Of course, what goes on in this factory is more complex than we've been letting on. Many of the best scientific brains in the world are trying to duplicate the photosynthesis factory. They're working on "artificial photosynthesis." No dirt, no trees, just chemicals like chlorophyll, carbon dioxide, and lots of light. Guess what? It doesn't work.

The real photosynthesis factory, like all factories, had to be designed by a master designer. Every step along the assembly line, from light energy to chemical energy (the glucose product), had to be planned. Who planned it? The Ultimate Master Designer—God. Thank God for making it happen.

From Paper to Ping-Pong Balls

You don't have to live in the forest to have trees all around you. They play a big part in your daily life. We use things like lumber, plywood, and paper every day. A great many other products start off as wood, bark, and even leaves. Be a wood detective and check off each item below that you think comes from trees (for the answer see page 153):

❏ Maple syrup
❏ Ink
❏ Clothing
❏ Raincoats
❏ Adhesives
❏ Plates
❏ Flashlight batteries
❏ Plaster
❏ Waxed paper
❏ Artificial stones
❏ Explosives
❏ Piano keys
❏ Pencils
❏ Movie films

❏ Dyes
❏ Molasses
❏ Laxatives
❏ Leather goods
❏ Bathroom tissue
❏ Cement
❏ Fuel for cars
❏ Milk cartons
❏ Soap
❏ Toothbrushes
❏ Sausage casings
❏ Shoes
❏ Insecticides
❏ Linoleum flooring

❏ Paint
❏ Recording tape
❏ Steering wheels
❏ Insulation
❏ Ping-Pong balls
❏ Charcoal briquettes
❏ Tires
❏ Hockey sticks
❏ Metal polishes
❏ Sponges
❏ Floor cleaner
❏ Skateboards
❏ Mountain climbers' packs

The Paint Factory

If you get excited about color, you can't help being tickled by the brilliant splashes of red, orange, and yellow in the October forest.

What makes the leaves change color? Surprisingly, the colors you see in the autumn were there all summer. You didn't see them because of that marvellous molecule—chlorophyll. In the summer, chlorophyll is very busy absorbing light, carbon dioxide, and water and turning them into food. In the fall, there's less sunlight. The days are shorter. The nights are longer. A lot of trees take a break from making chlorophyll and food.

When that happens, the other *color chemicals* (*pigments*) in the leaves start to show through. There's stuff like xanthophyll (yellow) and carotene (carrot orange) that become visible because there's less chlorophyll to hide them. Check it out.

What You Need:
- Green plant leaves.
- A tall drinking glass.
- Clear nail polish remover (acetone).
- A coffee filter.
- A pair of scissors.
- A pencil or chopstick.
- A measuring teaspoon.
- Adhesive tape.

What You Need To Do:
Get a few green leaves and tear them into the smallest pieces you can. Use a spoon to mash your leaf bits until you have a good mush. Sometimes this works better if you add a pinch of sand. Put your mush into the bottom of a tall drinking glass and very slowly add 6 teaspoons of acetone. Wait 20 minutes to let the plant mush sink to the bottom of the glass. Cut a rectangle from your coffee filter. Tape it to the pencil so it hangs down into the glass and just touches the acetone but not the plant mush. Let the glass sit for 3 hours.

What Do You See?
Color. Acetone breaks down the structures (chloroplasts) that hold the pigments in place and releases them. The green is chlorophyll. The other colors spreading out on the paper are the other pigments, like xanthophyll and carotene, that you see when leaves change colors in the fall.

Now, who would have put these pigments in trees in the first place? Right! God! Not only are they beautiful, they work. Without the pigments the photosynthesis factory shuts down. No food. No life.

1.
2.
3.
4.

Note: Contents of glass have been enlarged to show detail.

Plant Babies

Trees *reproduce* other trees like themselves. Pine trees' children are baby pine trees, oaks tend to have oaks, hemlocks have hemlocks, and so on and so forth. You get the point. Truth is, all living things, not just trees, reproduce like this. Good thing, actually. When you plant carrots in the garden, it would be a real pity if up popped a head of cauliflower. When your pet cat had babies, how many of them grew up to be dogs? No, God seems to have had a reason for keeping one kind of living thing (what biologists call a *species*) distinct from other living things.

See for yourself. Grow something.

What You Need:

- Seeds. You should be able to find lots of cool seeds in your kitchen cupboards. Get your parents' permission first, but see if you can find some dried beans and peas, some spices such as herb seeds, coriander, fennel, and mustard, or the seeds from various fruits and vegetables. It might prove interesting to try some hamster and bird seed as well.
- Containers such as old yogurt cups.
- Soil for large seeds such as beans, and cotton wool for the teeny tiny seeds.

What You Need To Do:

Put soil in some of your containers and cotton wool in others. Moisten with a bit of water. Sprinkle some of the small seeds on the damp cotton wool. Bury some of the larger seeds about a fingernail deep in the dirt. Label the containers and wait for the seeds to begin growing. How long it takes will depend on what seeds you use, but you should begin to see new life within a day or two.

While you're waiting, take a moment to hold a seed. Got one? Think about this tiny miracle in your hand. Do you think you could make such a seed? Someone did. Someone who loved life very much and wanted to see it reproduce. That someone was the Creator, and he sure must have known what he was doing.

Smart Plants

Watch a sunflower some day. Its head *follows the sun* from sunrise to sunset. It's watching the sun so that it gets the most light it can. Do you think your bean plants from the last activity are as smart?

What You Need:

- A freshly sprouted bean plant from the last activity. Or grow a new one.
- A cardboard box that has cardboard dividers. See your friendly neighborhood produce manager for an apple box if you don't have something suitable.
- A pair of scissors.
- Masking tape.
- An adult to help.

What You Need To Do:

Have an adult help you cut out a maze through the dividers in the cardboard box by cutting holes in the dividers about 2 inches across. Make one hole in the outside wall of the box as well. Water your plant and place it in the farthest corner of the box from the outside hole. Place the box with the outside hole facing a sunny window. Close the lid and tape it to be sure that no light can enter the box except through the outside hole. Every few days you will need to open the box and water your plant.

What Do You See?

Your plant has successfully negotiated the maze! Plants grow towards sunlight. Remember the pigments? Chlorophyll can only make food if it can get sun. Your plant will twist and turn through the maze until one day you will see leaves poking through the outside hole. Smart plant.

Check This Out:

Do you know that the roots of plants are equally as smart as the stems? If you were to grow one of your seeds in a deep, clear container and turn it through 90º every 4 days, on its side, upright, upside down, etc., you would notice that the root growth would change direction as well. Try it. Roots will always grow downwards, toward water and the nutrients they need in the soil.

Toolbox: Facts and Superstitions

"Fascinating! Do you know what I just read, Dr. Lenslo?"

"Nope, but I have a feeling you're about to tell me."

"People used to believe that the Earth was held up by three elephants resting on the back of a giant turtle."

"Is that a fact, Dr. Paige?"

"That's what's soooo amazing. You see, it's a fact that I just told you what people used to believe. But what they believed wasn't a fact at all. It wasn't the truth."

"People sometimes think a lot of silly things. Not just people who lived a long time ago," Dr. Lenslo commented.

"Good point. What we call superstition used to be fact for a lot of people," Dr. Paige explained. "Folks used to 'know' that the Earth was flat, that the sun revolved around the Earth, and that rain fell through holes in heaven from a huge water tank in the sky."

"Silliness!" exclaimed Dr. Lenslo. "The Earth is round, it revolves around the sun, and rain falls from clouds of water vapor. Those are the facts!"

"How do you know, Dr. Lenslo?"

"Evidence. Scientists and their helpers, like me, have designed experiments to answer such questions. We've looked at the Earth and done science with it. We can trust our results because God made everything to follow the rules. Light travels in straight lines, air pressure pushes in all directions, plants grow toward the light . . . facts based on evidence."

"Exactly, my good Doctor," Dr. Paige agreed.

Wanna Try It?

Which of the following are facts? (Check your answers on page 153.)

1. Handling toads causes warts.

2. Dragonflies sting.
3. The bite of a tarantula is fatal (causes death).
4. The light of the moon affects crop growth.
5. The dodo bird is a huge, flightless relative of pigeons that lives on islands in the Indian Ocean.
6. Mules have never been known to have babies.
7. There is a rule you can learn to safely tell poisonous from non-poisonous mushrooms.
8. Girls are smarter than boys.
9. If I drop a cannonball and a golf ball at the same time from the same height, the cannonball will hit the ground first.

Elementary, My Good Doctor

Land is a mixture of a whole lot of matter. But what is matter made of? *Molecules*. The atmosphere is made of molecules. The land and oceans are made of molecules. To get this idea of molecules, it might help to realize that there are as many molecules in a spoonful of water as there are spoonfuls of water in the Atlantic Ocean.

The question is, what are molecules made of? Take table salt, for example. Scientists like you and me call table salt *sodium chloride*. Sodium chloride is a molecule made up of simpler chemicals called *elements*. Sodium and chlorine are both elements. Sodium is a shiny, butter-soft metal that explodes when put in water. Chlorine is a thick, green gas. Both elements are poisonous!

But when sodium and chlorine are mixed together, the elements hook together into a completely new chemical that we can eat. In fact, we have to eat a small amount of sodium chloride every day to keep our muscles and brains working properly. Salt does more, however, than just keep us alive. Salt is an important part of the science of chemistry.

Want to impress your family and friends with your scientific knowledge?

Salt Cleaner

What You Need:
- Old pennies.
- A jar with a lid.
- A measuring teaspoon.
- Salt.
- Vinegar.

What You Need To Do:
Put the pennies in the jar. Cover the pennies with vinegar. Add a teaspoon of salt. Put on the lid and shake. Rinse your pennies in clear cold water.

What Do You See?
The pennies become shiny and clean. Vinegar is really just a 5% or less solution of water and acetic acid. In the presence of this acid, the sodium and chlorine in the salt molecule don't hold on to each other as tightly. The chlorine goes after the copper in the pennies and scrubs it clean. When chemicals do this kind of work, we call it a *chemical reaction*. Rinsing our pennies in clean water stops the reaction.

Chemical reactions like these do a lot of work for us. The energy that we use to heat our homes, move our cars, and make just about everything around us all comes from chemical reactions designed by a master chemist, God himself.

Salt Lift

What You Need:
- A nice restaurant.
- A small piece of string.
- A glass of water with ice.
- Salt.

What You Need To Do:
Next time you're all sitting in a restaurant waiting for your meal to arrive, announce that you're going to lift an ice cube out of your drinking water using a short piece of string but without touching the ice with your fingers. See if anyone wants to try it. Before everyone gets frustrated

and starts spilling drinking glasses, demonstrate your solution to the puzzle: Lay your string across the ice cube and sprinkle salt from a salt shaker on top of the ice. Wait a minute or two. Lift your piece of string up.

What Do You See?

The ice cube sticks tightly to the string! The salt causes the ice around the string to melt. But in doing so, it will lose heat (which is another way of saying it will get colder) and the salt water will freeze again.

There is a lesson here for anyone who sprinkles salt on an icy sidewalk. Unless you use enough salt to melt all of the ice, the water will freeze again.

Here's another use for sodium chloride.

Trivia

Salt, the Seasoning of Life. Plain old salt, the humble seasoning you sometimes take for granted at mealtimes, has quite a history. People have fought wars over it, explored faraway lands in search of it, and built cities to be close to it. The word "salary" is a reminder that Roman soldiers were given a "salarium," or allowance, to buy salt.

White Powders

Everything in the universe is made up of a little more than 100 basic elements like sodium and chlorine. Other elements are oxygen, hydrogen, calcium, and iron. Think of elements as God's kitchen supplies. Let's see, two parts hydrogen to one part oxygen? Let's call it *water*. One part carbon to two parts oxygen? *Carbon dioxide.*

This isn't the same as going into your kitchen and throwing stuff together in hopes of creating a masterpiece for your tastebuds: a cup of sugar, a bit of salt, a little vinegar, chocolate sprinkles, perhaps some spinach . . . stir, mash, and bake. What do ya have? Yuuuck!

Fortunately, God had a recipe. God knew how much of each element to combine with just the right amount of other elements to end up with absolutely every bit of matter in the universe. To do this, he had to know every element's properties. *Properties* are like signatures. No two people have the same signature, and no two elements or molecules have the same properties. Properties include: state (solid, liquid, or gas), color, texture (rough, gritty, smooth), pH (see the next pages), solubility (does it dissolve in water?), and melting point and boiling point (useful properties, but you don't have the equipment to test these).

For example, not all white powders are created equal.

What You Need:
- Ground-up aspirin.
- Ground-up white chalk.
- Powdered sugar.
- 3 glasses of water.
- 3 spoons.
- A friend.

What You Need To Do:
With your parents' permission, place the powders in 3 small piles. Ask your friend to discover which one is chalk dust.

A couple of rules:
1. *Don't give in to temptation. Never taste any chemicals unless an adult you trust tells you to.*
2. *Before you try anything fancy, check with an adult.*

If your friend is smart, he or she will spoon the powders into separate glasses of water and stir.

What Do You See?
Two of the powders dissolve. One doesn't. This is chemical detective work. Which powder is insoluble in water? Right! Chalk. Good work!

Acids

Aspirin is a simpler name for the humungous (impress your parents) chemical name acetylsalicylic acid. Aspirin originally was made from parts of the willow tree. Of course, those little white pills don't look like willow bark, but they do contain the good stuff that God put in the tree to help you deal with the discomfort of fevers.

Soon after acetylsalicylic acid was discovered and offered to people as a pain reliever, people complained it left them with a stomach that felt "hot" or "raw." If you look at the chemical name for aspirin you can see why. Aspirin is an *acid*.

If you've ever sucked on a lemon (citric acid) or mixed too much vinegar (acetic acid) in your salad dressing, you know what mild acids are. Strong acids, such as hydrochloric acid or sulphuric acid, you want to stay well away from. Strong acids can burn the skin and even dissolve metals. Acetylsalicylic acid is between the mild and the strong acids, but it's strong enough to irritate the walls of your stomach.

Scientists love numbers. In fact, many would say the language of science is mathematics. One reason for this is that it allows them to be far more exact about such things as acids and bases. Just as there is an inch or metric ruler to measure exact lengths, there is a chemical ruler to measure the strengths of acids and their opposites, bases. That ruler is called *pH*.

The pH ruler runs from 0 (strong acids) to 14 (strong bases). Exactly in the middle is a pH of 7. Scientists call this *neutral*.

There are a great many ways of testing a substance to check its pH. One of the most interesting is to use another chemical that changes color at various pHs. These chemicals are called *indicators*. You may have used one at

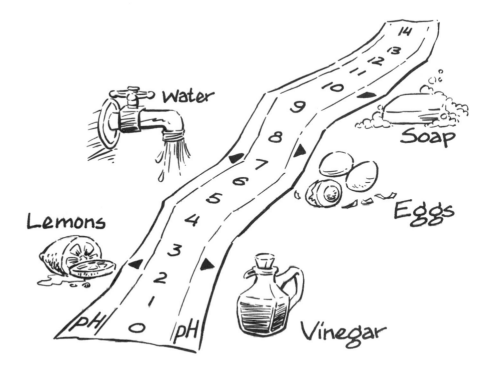

school by the name of litmus. It was probably dried into little strips of blue paper that turned red when you touched it to acid. Want to make your own? Turn the page.

Trivia

Aspirin was first made for medical use in 1893. It's still the leading pain killer and the usual treatment to reduce fever and swelling. Over 30 million pounds of aspirin (150 tablets per person) are used in the United States each year. Worldwide yearly use exceeds 100,000 tons.

pH: Make Your Own Indicator

You can make your own *acid/base indicator* out of some rather bizarre everyday ingredients.

What You Need:

- Purple cabbage.
- Water.
- A knife and a cutting board.
- A saucepan.
- A sieve.
- A large jar and some small jars.
- Substances to test: vinegar, lemon juice, cream of tartar, tap water, baking soda, ammonia, eggs, and soap.
- Adult help.

What You Need To Do:

Chop your purple cabbage into fine pieces. Boil a quart (liter) of water carefully in your saucepan. Add the chopped purple cabbage and after a minute take the saucepan off the heat. Let it stand for an hour until it's completely cool. Strain the liquid into a large jar and throw away (or eat) the used cabbage. The liquid should be a dark reddish purple color that will change when you add an acid or a base. You will know you have an acid if it changes to red and a strong base if it turns green. Weaker bases will change the cabbage juice to blue. With neutral substances, the indicator will remain purple.

Pour a small amount of your cabbage juice indicator into several small jars. To test if something is acid or base, add a little of the substance to one of your small jars.

Are acids and bases useful? For sure. The truth is we can't live a minute without them. You're surrounded by them. In the kitchen you'll find baking powder and baking soda (both bases) and vinegar and fruit juices (weak acids). From the above activity you know that most cleaners are strong bases.

You even find acids and bases inside your body. You would never eat another steak if it weren't for the presence of hydrochloric acid in your stomach. Life inside and outside your body depends on keeping the right levels of acids and bases. God designed creation to live in balance at just the right level of each. Acid rain wasn't a problem in the beginning; neither was acid indigestion. A lot of things have changed on planet Earth since God created it.

The Little Guys . . . Again

Cooking probably began as a way of delaying spoilage. Leave a plate of leftovers lying around for a few days and your nose will soon tell you that something dreadful has happened. The smelly mush that remains is not only unappetizing, it can make you very ill. This nasty change in your dinner can be blamed on *germs*. Want to grow some?

What You Need:
- 3 glasses of equal size.
- Vinegar, salt, and warm water.
- 3 beef bouillon cubes.
- A teaspoon measure.

What You Need To Do:
Fill all three glasses with warm water. Add a beef bouillon cube to each glass. Add a teaspoon of vinegar to one glass and a teaspoon of salt to another glass. Don't put anything else in the third glass. Place all three glasses in a sunny window for a week.

What Do You See?
Well, you're not going to see germs unless you have a good microscope available. What you will probably observe, however, are large groups or colonies of germs in the glass that had neither salt nor vinegar. The millions of bacteria should make the water cloudy, smelly, and definitely unfit for drinking.

But what about the vinegar and salt glasses?

Those should be clear. Vinegar and salt keep germs from growing. God put just the right amount of salt in our oceans to keep them from getting as disgusting as the glass of polluted water you just made. If you were to do a little research into food preservatives, you would see that in Bible days (days before canning, freezing, and refrigerating) salt and vinegar were the most important ways of keeping your food from going bad. Pickles, sauerkraut, and beef jerky are safe to eat because salt and the acid in the vinegar kill germs before they can grow.

Check This Out:
Try the same experiment, but add other substances to the water and beef bouillon. Can you find other things that kill the germs? What does orange juice do? Milk? Cola?

Had Your Goose Guts Today?

Germs (*bacteria*) cause nasty diseases. The proper hygiene that you take for granted . . . washing your hands with soap and water and using a toilet . . . was unknown 200 years ago. Even in big cities, people just threw human waste in the streets. This filth provided a smorgasbord for flies and bacteria to reproduce and spread disease.

A lot of suffering could have been prevented had people trusted the science God told Moses about. Moses gave us God's directions for killing bacteria by hand-washing. They sound very close to how today's doctors wash their hands before an operation.

The soap Moses used is even more amazing. It was made by burning together a young cow, cedar wood, hyssop branches, and wool. This amazing recipe contains an irritant to encourage scrubbing (cedar-wood oil); an antiseptic (hyssop oil) to kill bacteria and molds; and a scrubbing agent (wool) to scrape off the dirt and bacteria!

Compare God's recipe for health given to Moses with a medical book, the Ebers Papyrus, written by Egypt's best scientists of that time, 1552 B.C. (Moses, who "was educated in all the wisdom of the Egyptians," may have studied it). Ever had a sliver of wood stuck in your finger? An Egyptian Ebers Papyrus doctor would have put worms' blood and asses' dung on the splinter. Since dung is full of bacteria, you would have put those bacteria inside your nice warm, moist injury to reproduce big time. Can you say "Infection"?

Several hundred remedies for diseases are offered in the Ebers Papyrus. They call for: guts of goose, tails of mouse, hair of cat, eyes of pig, and toes of dog. Quite a prescription for health.

Which of these prescriptions worked? The science of the best brains in Egypt or the science of Moses? Right you are . . . the words God gave Moses. If Moses was telling the truth about health and disease, isn't it likely he was speaking the truth about God's creation? Seems to me people should have trusted him a long time ago and avoided a great deal of suffering. God speaks the truth. Count on it.

The Good, the Bad, and the Tasty

Not all bacteria are bad. They do interesting things to foods: Milk becomes cheese, a flour and water paste rises and becomes bread when baked. Many of these changes are produced by one-celled plants called *yeasts*. Yeasts belong to a group called *fungi*. Unlike green plants, they don't contain a food factory. No chlorophyll. No photosynthesis. They get their food from their surroundings.

What foods do yeasts eat? What do they produce as wastes? Good questions. Ready?

What You Need:

- Adult help.
- Water.
- A package of dry yeast.
- A measuring cup.
- 3 small glasses.
- A candy thermometer.
- A large pot.
- 3 spoons.
- Measuring spoons.
- Sugar, corn syrup, and cornstarch.

What You Need To Do:

Dissolve the yeast in ½ cup of 90ºF water. Divide this mixture equally into the glasses. Make a warm water bath in the large pot with 90ºF water. Put in enough water so the glasses can sit in it without water spilling into them. Put 1 tablespoon of sugar in the first glass, 1 tablespoon of corn syrup in the second, and 1 tablespoon of cornstarch in the third. Stir each glass with a different spoon. Put the glasses in the warm water bath and look for bubbles.

Which glass produces bubbles first? Which makes the biggest bubbles?

What Do You See?

Yeasts, like all living organisms, have to eat. They eat glucose, the product of the plant factory. Corn syrup comes

from corn plants (no kidding!), so it contains glucose. When yeasts munch on glucose (what people in the know call *fermentation*), they produce by-products the yeasts consider wastes. However, we find these "wastes" helpful. One is carbon dioxide. It's the bubbles given off first by the corn syrup set-up. The other two produce carbon dioxide more slowly. Reason? Starch and sugar are more complicated molecules and take longer to break down.

Who cares? Unless you like your bread paper thin (and tough as shoe leather), you care. The carbon dioxide gas makes bread rise. Warm, airy bread from the oven . . . all because the Creator designed some wee plants for a purpose.

Joke: What did one mushroom say to the other mushroom? Answer: You're sure a fun-gi.

Floating in the Salty Sea

Salt water is heavier than fresh water. It's a fact. But don't trust me. Weigh 4 cups of fresh water and compare it to the weight of 4 cups of salt water. What did I tell ya? Salt water has more stuff in it (salt) than fresh water. Another way of saying this is to say that salt water is denser than fresh water. No, this isn't a put down. *Density* is another property of matter like the one you used to tell the white powders apart.

The density of fresh water, for example, is 62.4 pounds per cubic foot (or 1 gram per cubic centimeter). Anything that floats in water (wood, cork, plastic) has a density less than this. Anything that sinks in water (rock, iron, lead) has a density greater.

Any idea what your density is? Well, you could go weigh yourself and divide this number by how much space you take up (your volume) to find out. But there is an easier way. Do you float in water? Just a bit, you say? Well then, your density is just slightly greater than the density of water.

Can an egg float in water? Try it!

What You Need:
- A clear glass (wider than an egg).
- An uncooked egg.
- Water.
- Salt.
- A teaspoon.

What You Need To Do:
Half fill your glass with water and carefully place the egg in the glass. Notice that the egg sinks in fresh water. Now start stirring salt into your glass 1 teaspoon at a time. Keep adding salt until the egg floats to the top of the glass.

Slowly fill the glass by carefully dribbling fresh water over a spoon held against the inside of it. This will keep the fresh water from mixing with the salt water. Don't shake or stir.

What Do You See?
You end up with the egg floating on the boundary between the fresh and salt water layers. Neat. Now you know why you float better in the salty ocean than in a fresh water lake. In lakes with lots of salt, like the Dead Sea, it's difficult to sink.

Making a Parfait of Color

A parfait is a tall, lip-smacking dessert built up with colorful layers of ice cream and assorted other cool treats. The science part of this definition is in the word *layers*. Based on what you know about density, it is possible to stack four layers of water one on top of the other. Want to give it a try?

What You Need:

- 4 short glasses and 1 tall (parfait) glass.
- Salt.
- Hot and cold water.
- 4 different food colors.

What You Need To Do:

Put cold water in 2 glasses and add salt to one of the glasses until no more will dissolve (we call this being *saturated*). Put hot water into the other 2 glasses and again add salt to one of the glasses until it too is saturated. Now, add a few drops of color to each glass so that you can tell them apart. To your tall glass, add the cold salt water followed slowly by the cold fresh water, then the hot salt water, and finally the hot fresh water. Providing you took care not to allow mixing, you should now have a parfait layered with 4 colors of water. Looks great, but I wouldn't suggest drinking it.

Check This Out:

If you had problems with mixing, you might want to try using 5 liquids that don't mix. Syrup, glycerol (available from a drugstore), water colored with red food coloring, olive oil or any light cooking oil, and rubbing alcohol (propanol) colored with blue food coloring. You definitely don't want to get your lips anywhere near this one, however.

Trivia

Osmium, a hard, bluish-white metallic element, is the densest substance known –1402.8 pounds per cubic foot.

Archimedes Saves a King some Gold: The ruler Hiero II asked Archie to find a method for determining whether a crown was pure gold or mixed with silver. Archimedes realized, as he stepped into a bath, that a given weight of gold would displace less water than an equal weight of silver (which is less dense than gold). He is said, in his excitement at his discovery, to have run home naked, shouting, "Eureka! Eureka!" ("I have found it! I have found it!").

Parting Shot

"Hmmmm. Me again. Dr. Lenslo. I've been thinking about those smart plants. Seems to me that plants aren't really all that smart after all. I mean seeds are great, but guess who does all the planting? People. If plants are so brainy, why don't they have a way of planting their own seeds?"

"I hear you," Dr. Paige responded. "Obviously plants can't walk around the neighborhood planting their seeds. Plants don't move. But hey, they do manage the next best thing. Trees such as apple trees wrap their seed in a fruit, then animals eat the fruit and carry the seeds to a new bit of soil. Plants let animals do the walking for them. Seems pretty smart to me."

"Okay," conceded Dr. Lenslo, "plants do some amazing things: food factories, smart stems and roots, hiding seeds in fruit. Where did they learn all this stuff? Must have had a super teacher."

"Yes, indeed. I'd say that they had the best teacher ever. The same teacher who provided the light and the atmosphere also provided the land. Interesting that you don't have plant life without all of these. Plants need the light and the carbon dioxide in the atmosphere for their food factories. But they wouldn't be able to actually make anything in the factory without roots being firmly attached to the land. It all comes down to matter and what's in it, my friend."

"You ever notice, Dr. Paige, how all of these very important things that God created—the light, the atmosphere, and the land—are all non-living and yet together they make life possible? It all fits together like a puzzle. The itty-bitty bacteria, the smaller-than-even-I-can-see molecules in the soil . . . all have an important job that God has given them to do."

"Same for the big stuff," Dr. Paige agreed. "Oceans of water, forests of trees, mountains of rock . . . without them, we don't have life."

"Let's face it, life must be really important to God."
"For sure!"

DAY 4

GOD MADE THE SUN AND THE MOON

Genesis 1:14–19: *Then God said, "Let there be lights* [stars and planets] *in the sky* [galaxy] *to separate day from night. . . ." And it happened. So God made the two large lights . . . to rule the day . . .* [and] *the night. He also made the stars. . . . God saw that all these things were good. Evening passed, and morning came. This was the fourth day.* (ICB; brackets added)

Space . . . the final frontier? Maybe for man. But God has "been there" and "done that" right from its beginning. Ever wondered how big space is or how many stars are out there? Any ideas how God got our universe started or keeps it going? What about life on other planets—should we expect an attack from Mars? Doctors Paige and Lenslo have pondered these and other questions. They want you to bravely go where no one has gone before to discover how the mysteries of space show our Creator's incredible genius at work, making it possible for us to experience life and all its wonders here on Earth.

Pretty cool, huh? We have a one-of-a-kind, designer universe because God loves us and wants to show us who he is. He not only wrote us an incredible record (the Bible) about his love, but he also backed it up with universal displays that are, literally, out of this world!

The Universe

Have you ever stopped to think how incredibly puny our world is compared to the rest of the *universe*? You haven't? Well then, let's pause a moment and do so. Scientists believe our galaxy (the Milky Way) is 100,000 light-years (see the Toolbox, page 76) across. That's 625,000 billion miles (a million billion kilometers)! With the use of powerful new telescopes, we're starting to get a glimpse of outer space and the billions of other galaxies beyond our own.

Getting back to our own galaxy—you know, Juice from Cows Avenue—our solar system is a mere speck about two-thirds of the way from the center of the Milky Way. The solar system has the sun at its center, and its farthest planet, Pluto, orbits the sun at a distance of approximately 3,750 million miles (6 billion kilometers). Remember, though, the galaxy is 650,000,000,000,000 miles across (1,000,000,000,000,000 km).

Solar Pop Can

How can we get some idea of how humungous the galaxy is compared to the solar system? I know. Let's say you're drinking a can of pop. If the top of the pop can were the solar system (not really, because if it were, then as you tried to drink you'd get pop all over Saturn and Mercury or, worse yet, you might get conked in the nose by Jupiter. Youch!) . . . Anyhow, if the top of the pop can were the solar system, the galaxy would be the size of North America! And to think the Milky Way is just one of BILLIONS of galaxies in the universe! Earth is like a freckle on a flea that is riding on a cow.

If we take a closer look at how the solar system moves in the galaxy and how all the planets interact, we realize God did more than make a funky light show for us to enjoy at night. As puny as the Earth may seem when we compare it to the rest of the universe, it is unique and the only perfect place for us to live. Consider the cool thoughts in this chapter about our planet's place in the universe.

The Sky in My Backyard

Ever been outside on a perfectly clear night and looked up to the sky? What did you see? Nothing? Well, take the blindfold off! Where were we? Oh yes, the night sky. Could you believe how many *stars* there are up there? Now, if you live in a large city, chances are, even if the sky was clear, you probably couldn't see many stars. There's just too much light from all the buildings and street lights bouncing off the particles in the air over the city. As a result, the stars appear quite faint, if you can see them at all. You have a couple of options at this point. One is that you can run an ad in your local newspaper requesting that everyone turn all their lights off the next time there is a really clear night. The other is to get out of the city and visit a more rural area. That way you'll get a really spectacular show. Wherever you go, take a little time for this one.

What You Need:
- A night when the sky is very clear.
- An old blanket.
- Appropriately warm clothing for the place you'll visit.
- A parent (plus anyone else who wants to get blown away by God's creation).

Optional:
- A pair of binoculars or a telescope.
- Popcorn for the show you're about to see.

What You Need To Do:

Stretch out on the blanket on your back. Get comfortable. Look all around above you. Don't try to figure too much out at this point. Just enjoy this part of God's creation for its beauty. Pick a small section of the sky and try to count the stars you see. If you brought a pair of binoculars with you, try counting the same area again. Notice how many more stars are visible using the binoculars? Now do the activity on the next page.

Pictures in the Night

"Twinkle, twinkle little star, how I wonder where you are . . ." hummed Dr. Lenslo.

"*Sigh!* Stars make me wonder too," replied Dr. Paige. "Uh oh! It's time to play NAME THAT INTERSTELLAR PHENOMENON!"

"Pheno-who??" asked Dr. Lenslo.

"Phenomenon!" answered Dr. Paige. "Something that appears, in this case, up in the sky. See if any of the events we can typically see from Earth are visible in the sky! Win fabulous prizes each time you correctly locate a constellation or spot an event in our prize categories! Prizes are subject to availability and your parents' permission."

"Oh boy, oh boy!" cried Dr. Lenslo. "I'm so excited I could jump out of the solar system!"

"Chill out, Dr. Lenslo!" said Dr. Paige. "Relax, and keep an eye out for shooting stars."

"Stars with guns?! Aaaaaaaaaaaah!"

"Just ignore him. Let's get on with our game!"

If you find:

The Big Dipper (Ursa Major): You win a ride on a moonbeam.

The Little Dipper (Ursa Minor): You win a trip at the speed of light.

Shooting star (meteor): You win a wish.

Meteor shower: You win a lot of wishes!

Satellite: You win one of Saturn's rings.

Pleiades (Seven Sisters): You win never seeing the inside of the bathroom again!

Orion: You win a bag of Oreo cookies.

Castor and Pollux (part of the Gemini group): You win a cruise with Paul (Acts 28:11).

Taurus: You win a trip to Spain.

The Milky Way: You win your very own cosmic cow.

A planet (They look like stars but don't twinkle and move across the background of stars): You win your very own Hubble telescope.

So, how did you do? Are you riding a moonbeam or off getting sized for your Saturn ring? If you have trouble spotting any of these night sky events, keep trying. More important than anything else is taking time to see how incredible the sky is. Knowing the God who put the whole universe in place is better than any game show prize could ever be!

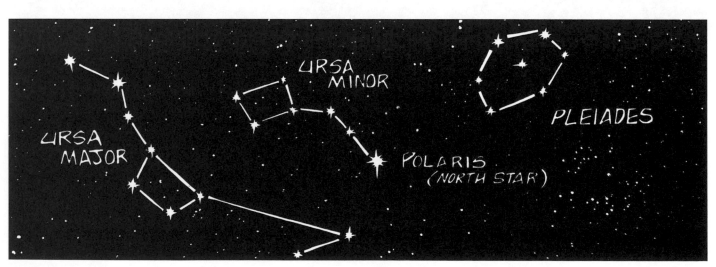

Slow Motion in the Sky

Have you ever tried to find the Big Dipper at different times on the same night only to find it had moved? Want to see why?

What You Need:

- A clear, starry night.
- A black umbrella.
- A package of star-shaped stickers (or any other small stickers that will show up).
- The constellation charts on page 68 (or another star chart you have from a science magazine or the Internet).

What You Need To Do:

Open the umbrella. On the inside, put a sticker on to represent the North Star (stick it near where the handle goes through the top of the umbrella). Place other stickers on for the other stars (if you have a very detailed star chart, just draw the major *constellations*) in their correct positions relative to the North Star. The Big and the Little Dippers (Ursa Major and Ursa Minor) are good ones to start with.

Once you've finished creating your starry, starry night, take it outside. Face towards *Polaris* (the North Star). Turn the handle of the umbrella until it lines up with Polaris and the constellations you've indicated on the umbrella match their actual

positions in the sky. Carefully set the umbrella on the ground. Leave it for an hour and come back.

What Do You See?

The stars have moved! When we look at the sky at different times on the same night it appears that the whole sky has rotated. Actually, it's the Earth that has rotated, spinning on its axis, making it seem like the stars have moved! The North Star is located almost directly above the axis of the Earth, so it doesn't appear to move.

Check This Out:

Try to predict where the stars will be in 2 hours. Rotate the umbrella counter-clockwise to where you think they will be and set it on the ground. Come back in 2 hours. How close was your prediction? Once you're finished, be sure to remove all the sticker stars off Umbrella Space!

Galaxy in a Cup

Here's your chance to make your very own *Milky Way*, in a cup!

What You Need:
- A cup of HOT coffee. (This can burn you, so be very careful. Also, don't drink it unless your mom and dad say it's okay because it will stunt your growth. Look at your parents. Oh. They're six foot four and six foot two? Hmmmm. Just think if they *hadn't* drunk coffee. They'd both be playing in the NBA! Ha! Ha!)
- A small pitcher of milk (or cream), preferably from a cosmic cow, but whatever kind your family has in the fridge will do.
- A teaspoon.

What You Need To Do:
Using the spoon, stir the coffee so that it's moving in a circular motion. Slowly pour a bit of the milk into the center of the coffee. Watch what happens.

What Do You See?
Assuming your milk was reasonably fresh and didn't fall in chunks to the bottom of the cup, the milk spread out in a spiral shape in the coffee.

You're not seeing a spiral? You say it looks more like Barney having a bad hair day, or even Elvis (ask your folks who he was—Thank you, thank you very much) on a mountain bike? Remember, this is a model AND it's science. We usually have to try a couple of times to get things right.

If we could go way out into space above our *galaxy*, it would appear as a huge spiral, like the one you saw in the cup of coffee, only there wouldn't be any milk involved. The Milky Way got its name because of how it looks from Earth when we look at it without a telescope: A long, great white cloud of tiny lights. We're talking massive numbers of stars swirling around in space like . . . like . . . milk in a coffee cup!

The Solar System

Remember the swirl of milk in the coffee cup? That was our galaxy, the Milky Way. Our *solar system* would be just a tiny speck about two-thirds of the way from the center of the swirl. Our solar system is unique. We have a star (the Sun) that is burning at just the right rate and is just the right distance away from us: It's close enough that we get enough heat and light but not so close that life is wiped out by the tremendous amount of energy the Sun produces. Although our solar system is enormous, it's the only known place in the universe to possess life. Even within our solar system, Earth is the only place suitable for life.

Ever have trouble remembering the order of the planets from the sun out to the farthest planet . . . which one is it again? Neptune or Uranus or . . . Pluto! That's it! Anyhow, we can use something called a mnemonic (nee-mon-ick) device. It's sort of like a power tool, only it's made out of words and helps us remember the names and order of other important words (remember Roy G Biv from Day 1?). Here goes:

Sunburned
Messy
Vikings
Eating
Mango
Jam
Sandwiches
Under
Nearby
Parasols.

Starting with the Sun, the first letter of each word in the corny sentence you just read stands for the first letter of the planets (Mercury, Venus, Earth, Mars, Jupiter, Saturn, Uranus, Neptune) all the way out to Pluto. For planets that have the same first letter, use the first two letters. Just picture a bunch of big red guys singing Swedish opera, wearing metal hats with horns on them, eating drippy jam sandwiches under pretty pink umbrellas. Okay, so it's a frightening thought, but now you can remember the order of the planets in our solar system, can't you!

A Trip through Our Solar System

How big is our solar system? REALLY BIG! There are 9 *planets* in it. The ones closest to the Earth are similar to Earth in that they are terrestrial—they are made up of materials similar to what the Earth is made up of and are solid. These include Mercury, Venus, Earth, and Mars.

The other five planets—the outer planets—are Jupiter, Saturn, Uranus, Neptune, and Pluto. All of the outer planets, with the exception of Pluto, are basically big balls of gas. Pluto is an oddity, being made of materials similar to what Earth is made up of.

The planets all orbit around the Sun in regular paths. The Sun is so large compared to any of the planets that they are held in these orbits by the Sun's gravity. Scientists are discovering new things about how important all the planets are for maintaining the conditions we have on Earth. Here's a way to get a sense of how big the planets are compared to one another and a way to get an idea of how far apart they are from each other.

What You Need:

- 10 recipe (file) cards, each one with the name of a planet on it (and one with "Sun" written on it).
- A basketball (or plastic grocery bag stuffed with crumpled newspaper to this size).
- 2 peppercorns.
- 3 pins with round plastic heads.
- A golf ball.
- A Ping-Pong ball.
- 2 marbles.
- A parent who likes to walk (or one who will at least pretend to like walking).

What You Need To Do:

The best place to do this activity is alongside a straight stretch of road that's just over a ¾ mile (1 km) long. You think *this* is a big laboratory! This is just a model that's on the scale of 1 to 5 billion. That means for every distance

of 1 (for example, 1 foot) you measure on your walk, you would have to measure 5 billion in space! Totally huge!

Anyhow, getting back to our walk. Place the basketball at the starting point and put the card that you wrote "Sun" on beside it. If you're concerned that the ball might be picked up by accident by someone who is not aware of the fact that it's actually a massive ball of burning hot gas, substitute it for something like a shopping bag stuffed full of crumpled up newspapers.

Pace off 11 giant steps (try to make sure each step is a little over 3 feet [1 m] long). Put one of the pins in the ground and place the card that has "Mercury" written on it beside it. You have now made a model that shows the relative sizes of the Sun and Mercury and how far from each other they are in relationship to their sizes.

Now take 10 giant steps and put one of the peppercorns down with the "Venus" card beside it.

Continue doing this as follows: 9 more steps and put the other peppercorn down with the "Earth" card, 15 steps and put another pin down with the "Mars" card, 110 steps and put down the golf ball with the "Jupiter" card, 131 more steps and put down the Ping-Pong ball with the "Saturn" card, 291 more steps and put a marble down with the "Uranus" card, 328 more steps and put the other marble down with the "Neptune" card. Finally, go 282 more steps and put the last pin down with the "Pluto" card.

You are now at the edge of the solar system, standing beside the farthest known planet from the Sun. You have also walked nearly 3,750 million miles (six billion kilometers)! Congratulations! Now let's go for a 3,750 million mile jog to pick up 9 planets and their name tags. Talk about an ultra marathon!

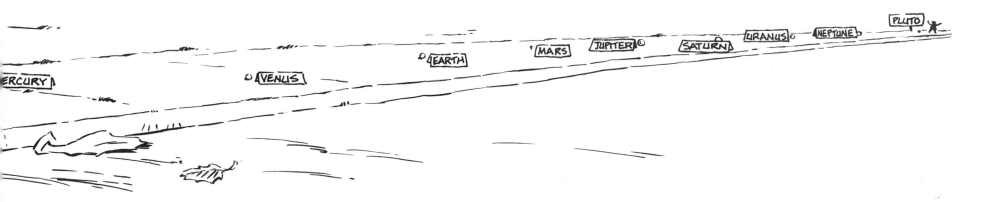

The Sun

The *Sun* is our solar system's star. It's 875,000 miles (1,400,000 km) in diameter and made up of mostly hydrogen gas and some helium. Its surface temperature is 5500ºC (about 9900ºF). We're talking enormously huge and hot! Earth is nearly 94 million miles (150 million km) away from the Sun which is the source of all our energy. Take a look.

Solar Peanuts

Remember the ultimate clean energy factory from Day 3? All green plants are specially designed with built-in solar panels in their leaves. The energy they capture is stored as different chemicals (fats, sugars, proteins, and starches) in other parts of the plant. Take the peanut, for instance. Its *chemical energy* is stored in the seeds (40–50% oil and 20–30% protein), which we can then eat. So you're not eating a peanut butter and jam sandwich; it's really a sunshine and jam sandwich.

What You Need:
- A well-ventilated area (outside or on your stove with the exhaust fan on).
- A soft-drink can.
- A cookie sheet.
- A paper clip.
- Shelled, raw peanuts.
- A box of matches.
- A coat hanger.
- A utility knife.
- A book.
- Adult supervision.

What You Need To Do:
Remove the pull tab from the soft-drink can. Bend the coat hanger into the shape of the stand shown. Place it on the cookie sheet and lay the book on top of the coat hanger's base so it doesn't tip. Carefully poke a hole in the can near the top rim. Fill the can ¼ full with cold water and hang it on the stand. Be sure there's about 2 inches (5 cm) clearance beneath the can.

Make a stand for the peanut out of the paper clip and place it in the center of the cookie sheet. Stand a shelled peanut on the stand (like a football you're going to kick, only don't kick this one or the experiment ends here!). Light a match and hold it under the peanut until it starts to burn. Put the can stand on the cookie sheet above the burning peanut. When the peanut stops burning, pour a bit of the water from the can over your fingers.

What Do You See?

The water is warm! The sunlight captured by the peanut plant was released as heat (and light) as the peanut burned. Stupendous!

Hot DOG! Making a Solar Weenie Roaster

What You Need:

- A shoe box (as deep as possible).
- A coat hanger.
- A sheet of aluminum foil about 12–18 inches (30–45 cm) long.
- A sheet of plastic food wrap.
- Tape.

What You Need To Do:

Poke a small hole halfway along each short edge of the shoe box, about 1 inch (2.5 cm) from the top. Line the inside of the box with the aluminum foil, but shape it as a smooth parabolic curve (like half an oval). You may need to try different curves until the light focuses on the wieners (see the next step). Straighten the coat hanger and push one end of it through one of the holes. Push one or two wieners (depending on the size of the shoe box) onto the coat hanger. Push the coat hanger a bit farther so it goes through the other hole poked in the shoe box. Cover the opening to the shoe box with the clear plastic food wrap and secure it tightly with tape.

Place the roaster in the sun so the front "window" faces the sun directly. Turn the wire every so often to ensure that the wieners roast evenly. Open the roaster when the wieners are cooked. How long this takes will depend on the time of day and how well your foil reflector is focused on the wieners. Enjoy your wiener in a hotdog bun lathered with ketchup and mustard and relish and . . .

This is one way of capturing the sun's energy. We call this *solar energy*. Actually, virtually all energy we have originates from the sun. For example, coal and oil come from plant and animal remains that have been buried in the ground for a long time. The plants got their energy from the sun and the animals, in part, got their energy from the plants. It's like sunlight stored under the ground, waiting to be used at a later time!

Toolbox: Numbers—The Language of Science

"Is a light-year some new diet soft drink?" inquired Dr. Lenslo.

"No, my focused little friend," answered Dr. Paige knowingly. "A light-year is the measurement used by astronomers and physicists for UNBELIEVABLY long distances. A light-year is the distance you could travel if you kept moving for a whole year at the speed of light."

"That's fast, isn't it, Dr. Paige?"

"You're not kidding! This is where the big numbers come in. Light travels at 187,000 miles per second (300,000 km/s). And this is where the math comes in. In one year there are 365 days, each having 24 hours, each hour having 60 minutes, and each minute having 60 seconds. If we multiply these together, we get 31,536,000 seconds in one year. Now, if we multiply the speed of light by the number of seconds in a year using a REALLY wide calculator . . ."

"I'd rather use my abacus!" interrupted Dr. Lenslo. "I just love flipping the beads around. I pretend I'm an ancient Chinese merchant, adding up my profits after a successful year of trade . . ."

"I'm happy for you. But I doubt you have enough beads, flip them as you might!" Dr. Paige said.

"Well, let's see," Dr. Lenslo said, flipping his beads. Flip, flip, flip. "I seem to be running out . . . Help!"

"ANYWAY, using our calculator—or better yet, a computer," Dr. Paige said meaningly, "we get the number 5,913,000,000,000 miles (9,460,800,000,000 km). Scientists usually round this off to 6 trillion miles (10 trillion km). That's a long way."

"Make sure you pack some soft drinks for the trip," Dr. Lenslo reminded Dr. Paige. "Try New *YEAR* lite: half the calories, but it's out of this world!"

"Aaaaaah!" Dr. Paige exclaimed, not quite in awe of Dr. Lenslo's talent.

"Okay, so it needs a little work. But you should hear it with the jingle . . . 'New YEAR *lite*! It's all right. Makes you real bright . . . ,'" Dr. Lenslo sang, bopping to his tune.

"Ahem," Dr. Paige sighed. "I'd rather you flipped your beads."

The Moon

The *moon*. It's the "smaller light" we read about in Genesis 1:16. Our moon isn't one of the planets in our solar system because, well, IT'S A MOON! It acts the same way a satellite we send into space behaves in the Earth's gravitational field. The moon orbits the Earth once every 29½ days at a distance of approximately 239,000 miles (384,000 km). Because it also rotates on its axis in the same amount of time, we only see one side of the moon from the Earth.

You and a friend can show this by having one of you walk sideways around the other one, making sure the person who is walking keeps facing forward. This person never has the back of his or her head to the person standing in the middle, just like the moon never shows its other side to the Earth.

The moon is 2,160 miles (3,480 km) in diameter (as compared to the Earth's diameter of 8,000 miles, or 12,500 km). The force of gravity on the moon is only ⅙ as strong as the force of gravity on the Earth. The moon deserves special mention here because it plays such an important role in maintaining the conditions we need on Earth for life. See how well you know the effects of the moon on the Earth.

Of Moon or Not of Moon? That Is the Question.

Below is a list of activities and events that occur on Earth. Which ones require the moon's influence? Once you've decided, check out pages 153–154 for the answers.

1. Brushing your teeth.
2. Using the Internet.
3. Windsurfing on a lake.
4. Strange animal behavior.
5. Bad hair days.
6. Marine animals feeding.
7. The Earth not being a perfect sphere (ball shape).
8. The force of gravity.
9. Surfing in Hawaii.
10. Using a vacuum cleaner.

Eclipses

"Egg lips?" Dr. Lenslo asked with surprise. "Why are we talking about egg lips? Everyone knows eggs don't have lips. Fish have lips. People have lips. Birds have lips. But eggs DO NOT HAVE LIPS!"

"Eclipses, my friend, *eclipses*, not *egg lips*!" Dr. Paige responded. "And since when do birds have lips? Where's the author, before this goes completely off track!"

There are two kinds of eclipses: a *solar eclipse* and a *lunar eclipse*. The first kind occurs when the moon passes between the Sun and the Earth, causing the moon's shadow to fall on the Earth. When viewed from Earth, the Sun appears to become temporarily darkened. The second kind occurs when the Earth passes between the sun and the moon, causing Earth's shadow to fall across the moon. From Earth, the moon appears to become temporarily darkened.

What You Need:
- A basketball.
- A softball.
- A flashlight.
- Books.
- A darkened room. I mean really dark!
- An assistant.

What You Need To Do:
The large ball—slam dunk!—will be the Earth. The small ball—swing batter!—will be the moon. Set the basketball on a table (put some books beside it if it tries to roll off the table). Have your assistant stand back from the table and shine the flashlight on the basketball. Hold the softball carefully with two fingers and slowly move it between the flashlight and the basketball.

What Do You See?
The shadow that falls across the basketball is similar to that which is cast on the Earth during a solar eclipse. Keep moving the small ball around the large ball until it's completely shadowed by the large ball. The shadow that falls across the small ball is similar to what happens during a lunar eclipse.

CAUTION: Never look directly at the Sun during a solar eclipse or at any other time! Doing so can cause blindness or permanent eye damage.

Cosmic Deli Moon Cheese

The moon is probably the most observed space body we can see from Earth. Because it's so close to the Earth compared to the planets, it appears to be huge. If you have ever observed a harvest moon in late September, you know that the moon looks even bigger as it rises on the horizon: It's a full moon and, compared to how it looks when it's high in the sky, it seems larger right next to the horizon. Have you ever heard someone say the moon looks like Swiss cheese, all full of holes? When astronauts traveled to the moon, they observed many *craters* of different sizes on the surface of the moon. The largest craters are nearly 185 miles (300 km) across. Let's find out how those craters got there.

What You Need:
- Moist sand (like the kind you'd find in a sand box).
- Flour.
- A cake pan (or any shallow container).
- A large rock (orange size) and a small rock (marble size).
- 2 pieces of string, each 2½ yards (1–2 m) long.
- Duct tape (optional).

What You Need To Do:
Put moist sand 2 inches (5 cm) deep on the bottom of the cake pan. Put a ½ – ¾ inch (1–2 cm) layer of flour on the sand. Tie one end of a string to the large rock (use duct tape to help hold it in place). Tie one end of the other string to the small rock. Drop each rock onto your "moon" from different heights. Carefully lift each dropped rock out of its "crater." Do this several times with each rock.

What Do You See?
How did the height from which you dropped the rocks affect the craters made?

The moon's surface is full of craters, big and small, made when chunks of space rock (*meteors*) smashed into the moon's surface. The size of the rocks and the speed they were traveling upon impact determined the size of the craters made.

Staying Grounded on Earth

An invisible force on every planet causes stuff on or near the planet to be attracted to it. The larger the planet, the greater this force. It's not magnetism. Give up? *Gravity*. Earth's gravity is perfect. If it were much less, we'd bounce along as we walked (like on the moon). If it were much greater, it would be hard to stand up. When the space shuttle blasts off, it has to use powerful rockets that not only can lift the space shuttle but can also overcome Earth's gravitational pull.

Want to defy gravity? Grab a couple of bungee jumpers and see how to safely enjoy the thrill of gravity.

What You Need:
- 1 or 2 10-inch (25 cm) tall, human-like dolls whose names rhyme with Karbie and Ben.
- A package of rubber bands.
- 2 yard-sticks or meter-sticks.
- Some heavy books or C-clamps.
- A large basin or bowl of water.

What You Need To Do:
Make bungee bridges by attaching the rulers to a table edge using the heavy books or C-clamps. The rulers should stick out about 12 inches (30 cm). Make 2 chains of rubber bands by linking them together end-to-end. Attach one end of each chain to a bridge and the other end to the ankles of your jumpers. Place the basin of water on the floor beneath the bridges. Do a test dive with either Karbie or Ben. The goal is to have them just dunk their heads in the water without hitting the bottom of the basin. IF:
- Karbie or Ben doesn't touch the water: add rubber bands to the chain.
- They hit the bottom of the basin: remove rubber bands.

What Do You See?
When Karbie and Ben fall, they're being pulled toward the water by gravity. Fortunately, the bungee cord pulls gradually in the opposite direction, keeping them from crashing and preventing a sudden jolt that using a regular rope would cause.

For a real challenge, try this off your balcony using Karbie and Ben and a really loooong rubber band chain. Warn anyone walking below of the bungee jumping competition in progress!

The Best Place in the Solar System

"Do you remember the story of the three bears and the inconsiderate young lady who tried ripping off their porridge?" Dr. Lenslo asked Dr. Paige.

"Why, yes, I do recall hearing about that incident," replied Dr. Paige. "Didn't the bears press charges for unlawfully causing harm to someone else's breakfast?"

"Indeed they did. However, they dropped the charges when they found out she was doing research for her science fair project on why Earth is the perfect place to live in our solar system," Dr. Lenslo explained. "In the end she found out that, like the last bowl of porridge she tried, Earth is just right compared to the other planets."

Here's a list of "What ifs?" about *Earth*. See if you can match them to the statements in the other column. (The answers are on page 154.)

What if . . .

Earth were any closer to the sun?
Earth's temperature were even a few degrees cooler?
Earth's temperature were even a few degrees warmer?
Earth rotated more quickly?
Earth rotated less quickly?

Earth didn't have a planetary neighbor the size of Jupiter?
Earth's moon were smaller?
Earth's moon were larger?

The result would be . . .

Huge tides flood coastal areas throughout planet.
Planet is cruelly battered by meteors and comet debris.
Ice floes grow by leaps and bounds; planet freezes.
Temperature differences between day and night prohibit life.
Huge greenhouse effect causes planet to boil.
Raging winds make life impossible.
No tides; shore and tidal critters die.
All life on planet is killed by radiation.

Our planet is special. Not only are the conditions on Earth perfect for supporting life, but conditions in the solar system and the galaxy beyond are incredibly fine-tuned to allow Earth's conditions to remain stable. Not a single mistake was made as God spun the universe into motion and being. Earth is truly a one-of-a-kind designer planet that is juuuuuust right!

Blast Off!

"Where are we going to go?" shouted Dr. Lenslo.
"Higher!" cried Dr. Paige.
"When are we going to get there?" asked Dr. Lenslo.
"Real soon!" Dr. Paige responded.

That's right, Dr. Lenslo and Dr. Paige. Time to slide into your astronaut suits and head to the stars. As humans, we have a deep longing to know who we are in the vastness of space. We also have a deep curiosity to know about our solar system. What else might be out there? Who else might be out there?

People have walked on the moon. This wouldn't have happened if the scientists involved had disobeyed any of the *laws of physics*. Here are a couple of activities that demonstrate some of these principles as well as principles of rocketry.

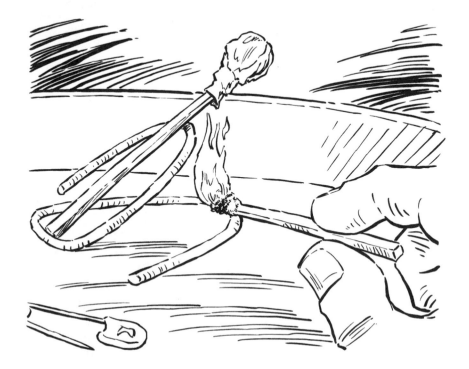

Match Rockets

What You Need:
- 2 matches.
- A 1-inch (2 cm) square of aluminum foil.
- A paper clip.
- A safety pin.
- An aluminum pie pan.
- An adult.

What You Need To Do:
CAUTION: Be sure you're working in an area where there are no flammable materials nearby. The best place is outdoors on a clear cement surface.

Shape the paper clip into the launch pad (see diagram) and place it in the center of the pie pan. Wrap the square of aluminum foil tightly around the head of one match, as shown. Use the safety pin to make a small opening between the foil and the match. Stand the rocket in the launch pad. Light the second match and use it to light the rocket by placing the burning flame just beneath the aluminum foil. Blast off!

Try it a couple of times. The way the match blasts off depends somewhat on how you wrap the foil.

What Do You See?
The exhaust of the burning match head escapes from the hole, pushing downward. The rocket reacts by being pushed upward. This demonstrates Isaac Newton's *third law of motion*: For every action, there is an opposite and equal reaction.

Two-in-One Rockets

When *rockets* (including the space shuttle) are sent into space, they require huge amounts of fuel. A lot of the fuel is needed to lift a lot of the fuel! To avoid using a single rocket, scientists use a method developed by a sixteenth-century fireworks maker named John Schmidlap. Rockets are ignited in stages to push the rocket and its fuel on to its destination. Let's try it using a balloon model that won't even require us to light a match!

What You Need:

- 2 drinking straws (the wider ones fast food restaurants provide).
- Fishing line (enough to reach across the room or between two trees).
- 2 long, round balloons (not the really skinny ones nor the chubby ones).
- A Styrofoam coffee cup.
- A pair of scissors.
- A clothespin.
- Adhesive tape (duct tape is best).
- An extra person to be your third and fourth hands!

What You Need To Do:

Thread the fishing line through the 2 drinking straws. Fasten the line to opposite sides of the room, just high enough so people can still walk under it and tight enough so it won't droop. Cut the Styrofoam cup in half, keeping the lip as a continuous ring. Inflate one balloon about ¾ full. Pinching the opening, pass it through the cup ring. Hand this to your assistant, having him or her pinch the opening.

Partially inflate the second balloon and push the tip of it through the cup ring from behind the first balloon, so it squeezes off the first balloon's opening. Fully inflate the second balloon. Twist the opening and pinch it off with a clothespin. Tape the balloons to the straws, as shown.

Move the balloons to one end of the fishing line track. Remove the clothespin. Blast off . . . and off again!

While we're rocketing off into space, will we ever find life on other planets or in other parts of the universe? The Bible doesn't say anything about this. However, from what scientists know at present, there is no other place like the Earth anywhere. We don't have to fear an attack from Mars!

Parting Shot

"How many stars do you think are in the sky?" asked Dr. Paige.

"Billions and billions!" Dr. Lenslo declared.

"Right! Scientists believe there are about one hundred billion (1 with eleven zeros after it) stars in the Milky Way."

"So that's why it looks so milky!"

"If every person on Earth claimed an equal share of these stars they would each get 15 to 16."

"Is that all?" Dr. Lenslo sighed.

"Well, check out the universe's 100 billion other galaxies. For every one of your stars from our galaxy, you would get a billion from other galaxies. We're talking stupendously enormous numbers of stars!"

"Numbers that big make my head hurt!" groaned Dr. Lenslo. "Where's my abacus?"

"Hold your beads! The Bible talks about this. Look up Genesis 26:4. The Bible also says each star is unique: *Also there are heavenly bodies and earthly bodies. But the beauty of the heavenly bodies is one kind. The beauty of the earthly bodies is another kind. The sun has one kind of beauty. The moon has another beauty, and the stars another. And each star is different in its beauty* (1 Corinthians 15:40–41, ICB)."

"You're saying the numberless stars are all unique!"

"Precisely! Nowhere else in the universe is there a star like our Sun. It's all part of God's plan for us to live on Earth."

"Will we ever see the outer limits of space?" inquired Dr. Lenslo.

"Probably not in our lifetime," answered Dr. Paige. "As technology improves, space probes will be sent to more distant planets and even to galaxies beyond the Milky Way. However, with billions of stars to explore so many light-years away, it's unlikely, even with greatly improved space travel, we'll ever visit most of the heavenly bodies we see at night."

"Hey! God's Word talks about how limitless the stars in the sky are," Dr. Lenslo exclaimed. "Check out Jeremiah 33:22: *But I will give many descendants to my servant David . . . . They will be as many as the stars in the sky that no one can count . . .* (ICB)."

By now you should be back on your blanket, gazing up at the sky. Imagine if we could see all the galaxies. Now that would be amazing beyond belief!

DAY 5

GOD MADE THE BIRDS AND THE FISH

Genesis 1:20–23: *Then God said, "Let the water be filled with living things. And let birds fly in the air above the earth." So God created . . . every living thing that moves in the sea. Each one produces more of its own kind. God also made every bird that flies. And each bird produces more of its own kind. God saw that this was good. . . . Evening passed, and morning came. This was the fifth day. (ICB)*

The fifth day on planet Earth is here. The stage has been set for an amazing cast of characters to be introduced to Earth. By now the land and the sea are full of all sorts of plant life, big and small. Habitats have been created to support what God had in mind next.

God didn't just create one or two kinds of birds and a couple of types of fish. Genesis 1 says the waters were teeming with fish. No, this doesn't mean that the Miami Dolphins and the Atlanta Hawks were already active in the NFL and NBA. It means that God demonstrates his infinite creativity in the creatures of the sea and the birds of the air. Let's take a closer look.

Building Blocks of Life: Cells

All living things are made up of *cells*, animals included. Cells are like the building blocks that come together to make the bigger unit of the organism. They're like the bricks used to make a building: They come in different shapes and sizes, but they share a common purpose—maintaining the creature they are part of. Cells in each tissue of an organism are designed for a specific function. Take a bird, for instance. One kind of cells make up the feathers. Other cells make up the muscles in the wings of the bird, allowing it to glide and soar. Still other cells make up the skin, providing a continuous covering for the whole body. Want to take a look at a cell?

See-Through Egg

What You Need:
- An egg.
- A jar (big enough to comfortably hold the egg).
- Vinegar (enough to cover the egg).
- A plastic pot scrubber.
- A large spoon.

What You Need To Do:
Place the egg in the jar. Pour vinegar over the egg until it's completely covered. Let it stand for at least 24 hours. Carefully lift the egg out of the jar using a large spoon. Touch the shell and see if it's soft. If some of the shell still remains, return the egg to the jar of vinegar and allow it to stand for several more hours. Carefully lift the egg out on a large spoon and *gently* scrub the surface using the plastic pot scrubber. Rinse under cold water.

What Do You See?

You can see the yolk of the egg suspended in the white. You now have a model of an animal cell. The yolk represents the cell's *nucleus*. It's kind of like a chemical library with all the instructions for what the cell makes. Outside the nucleus is the *cytoplasm* (sight-o-plas-m). This is represented by the white of the egg in our model. This is where various substances are made, including proteins and other cell building materials. Finally, we have the shell *membrane* of the egg. This is the outer layer of the cell. It allows some substances to pass in and out of the cell while it blocks other substances from entering.

All cells share the common characteristics of nucleus, cytoplasm, and cell membrane. Cells of different tissues can vary in shape and size depending on what each was designed to do.

One of the jobs cells have is to make the concentrations of substances on both sides of their membranes even. To do this, cells absorb water by a process called *osmosis*. The absorbed water dilutes substances that are too concentrated.

Parts of a Cell

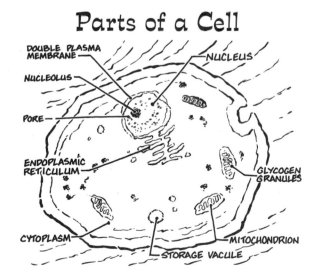

DOUBLE PLASMA MEMBRANE
NUCLEUS
NUCLEOLUS
PORE
ENDOPLASMIC RETICULUM
GLYCOGEN GRANULES
CYTOPLASM
MITOCHONDRION
STORAGE VACULE

Potato Sponges

What You Need:

- 2 medium-sized potatoes.
- 3 shallow dishes.
- A pot of boiling water.
- A sharp knife.
- Cold water.
- Salt.
- A teaspoon.
- Adult supervision.

What You Need To Do:

Cut the potatoes in half. (You can throw one potato half away.) Boil one potato half in the pot of water for 10 minutes. This kills the cells. Put about ½ cup (125 ml) of cold water in each dish. Carefully remove the potato half from the boiling water and place it cut side down on one of the dishes. Place two of the other potato halves on the dishes, one dish each, cut side down.

Scoop out a small depression in the top of each potato, being careful not to dig right through the potato. Leave one raw potato as your control—no salt (see page 125). Place 1 teaspoon of salt in the depressions of each of the other potatoes—the cooked potato half and the other raw potato half. Watch what happens.

What Do You See?

The raw potato with the salt absorbs water into its cells by osmosis to try and reduce the concentration of salt in the depression. The cooked potato, however, is no longer able to absorb water by osmosis because its cells were killed when it was cooked.

What's for Dinner, Chez Ocean?

"Captain Paige, we're being attacked! Dive! Dive!"

"What are you talking about? We're perfectly safe in our Sea Observation Submarine, Navigator Lenslo."

"I know. It's just . . . I've always wanted to say that!"

"Now that you've got that out of your system, let's put your skills of keen observation to work for our next job."

The ocean holds a wealth of variety in animal life. Some of the creatures we find in the ocean are among the largest ones inhabiting Earth. Then there are ones so tiny they can barely be seen without a microscope; yet there are so many of them that they outweigh all the other sea creatures combined.

Ultimately the sun provides all the energy on Earth, including that used by organisms in the sea. Each organism plays a part in the undersea community. Most organisms are considered to be food to some other organism somewhere along the way. When we consider what animals eat, and what eats those animals, we begin to create *food chains*. When we put several food chains together and look at links between the different chains, we get a *food web*. Try this next activity to make your own food chain. Bon appetit!

What You Need:
- Your brain with your imagination switched on to high.
- Several rolls of fruit leather.
- Toothpicks.
- A pair of scissors.

What You Need To Do:
Roll out the fruit leather so that it lies flat. Using a toothpick, sketch the critters from the list below (some are shown in the picture on page 88) on the rolls of fruit leather. Using the scissors, cut out each critter.

Sea gull	Plankton (phyto- and zoo-)
Bald eagle	Starfish
Orca (killer whale)	Crab
Seal	Shrimp
Salmon	Sea anenome
Red snapper	Clam
Herring	Octopus
Sea weed	

Now, invite them to dinner. Pick one of them to be your main dinner guest. Pick the sea critters that guest would eat and place them on one side of it. Now think about what critters would consider your first dinner guest to be a tasty option on their daily menu. Place them on the other side of your first guest. (What determines if one critter can use another critter as a source of food?)

See if you can extend your diagram to include critters that would be eaten by guest #1's food and critters that would eat what's eating guest #1!

What Do You See?
What you've created is the beginning of a 3-D food chain diagram. Usually the organisms at the bottom of the chain have the largest populations. And organisms at the top of a food chain are fewer.

Now, eat your way down the food chain. Yes, eat the starfish and anemones, too. The whole food chain is important. If you neglected to eat one organism, just think of the problems! They'd keep increasing their numbers until they took over the ocean, the world, the UNIVERSE! So eat up.

The variety of creatures in the sea shows God's imagination for design as well as the way he provides for every creature.

Shocking Sharks

Sharks have a reputation for being ferocious killers. While they do feed on a variety of fish and mammals, they're also scavengers, eating dead creatures and even garbage from ships. Sharks are particularly sensitive to sounds of low frequency and have fine directional hearing. They also have an excellent sense of smell, allowing them to sense very tiny amounts of substances in the water. This lets them follow, say, a trail of blood coming from a wounded animal.

While their sense of smell helps (they have very weak eyes), sharks are also equipped with another unique sense: They can pick up the weak electrical signals from the movement of muscles in nearby fish! They have special organs in various parts of their bodies that detect these signals. Electrifying, isn't it?

Pump It Up: Muscle in the Mussels

Whoosh! Boom! Waves pounding, smashing, crashing against the rocky shore. While many sea critters scramble to stay afloat or seek shelter, the calm, cool, collected mussels nonchalantly weather the onslaught of the waves. Their secret? *Secretions*! Secretions are gluey stuff the mussel makes so it can stick to the rock, even under water. A mass of tiny, stringy threads, with a protein superglue, is the secret.

Scientists are trying to duplicate what the mussel has been able to do ever since God put mussels in the oceans. The uses for such a glue would be endless, from mending broken bones to patching leaking ship hulls. Want to take a shot at it?

What You Need:

- Flour, water, sugar, honey, eggs, or any other cooking supplies you think might help make a good glue. This is a great chance to experiment! Be sure to ask your parents' permission before using anything in the kitchen.
- A bowl or jar to mix your glue in.
- A selection of hard materials, such as wood, plastic, and stone. Have 3 or 4 samples of each.
- A large basin or tub of water.
- Optional: newspapers to catch any drips of glue.
- A stick or brush to apply the glue with.

What You Need To Do:

Lay newspapers over the area you're planning to work in or work outside. Mix together your ingredients. Remember, glue needs to be sticky but not too wet. Glue together various combinations of the hard materials (wood to wood, wood to stone, plastic to stone, etc.). Allow the glue to dry thoroughly. Put the glued objects in the container of water. After 15 minutes, remove them and try to pull them apart. If you can't do it easily, put them back in the water for another 15 minutes. See which one will stay attached for the longest time.

What Do You See?

How'd they do? Any of them have the muscle of mussels?

People have made some amazing discoveries and produced many useful materials we use every day. But we can't make a glue like the mussels. God equipped every organism with all the right stuff to survive in the place it was created for.

Did Sid the Squid Flip His Lid?

The squid is a fascinating creature. Not only is it considered a delicacy by both people and beasts, it has some amazing *adaptations* to help it avoid being eaten every time its predators get the munchies. Like the octopus, the squid can release an inky substance into the water, creating a murky cloud and allowing it to quickly swim away, leaving the predator to check with the waiter for other options on the menu. The squid has a large *mantle* (it makes the squid look like it's wearing a big cone-shaped hat) that is very muscular. By squeezing the muscles in the mantle, the squid is able to quickly force water out of its body cavity, propelling it forward at high speeds. Let's try an experiment to demonstrate this.

What You Need:
• Loooong, skinny balloons (the ones that can be tied into animals, etc., work best).
• A bathtub ¼ full of water.
• A faucet that you can fit the opening of the balloon over.
• A pair of scissors that you can get wet.

What You Need To Do:
Partially fill several balloons with water (once you try one you will definitely want to do it again!) and tie off the openings. These are your squid. Lay your first squid at one end of the tub, pointing at the opposite end, with the tied end in your fingers. Carefully cut the end off and let it go.

To add to the squid get-away effect, have someone drip a bit of dark food coloring in the water as you release the squid. Similar to how the squid is able to squeeze water out of its mantle through the tubular siphon structure, the balloon squeezes the water out of the opening, propelling the balloon forward.

Check This Out:
Try putting dark food coloring in the water you fill your squids with. Get a friend to use a different food coloring in his or her squid. Have squid races. Who evades the predator best? What color makes it easier to hide the squid?

Something Fishy

What You Need:

- Different colors of modeling clay (see our non-hardening modeling clay recipe on page 155).
- A piece of cardboard to make your model on.

What You Need To Do:

Get a good-sized lump of clay. Roll and mold it into the shape of a fish. Give your fish a name. How about Sylvester? No? Okay, choose one that's a bit more fishy. Bubbles? Make Bubbles ⅛ inch (0.5 cm) in thickness. Using the diagram, mold Bubbles's different organs out of your clay. Use different colors so you can tell the different parts from one another in the completed model. As you make each part, place them on Bubbles in the correct location. As you place each of Bubbles's *organs* on the model, consider its function in survival.

Liver: helps purify Bubbles's blood and provides digestive juices.

Swim bladder: keeps Bubbles from sinking to the bottom. Our friend Bubbles adjusts the amount of gas (oxygen and nitrogen) in the bladder to go to the desired depth. (For more on this see page 103.)

Stomach: helps break down the food in the process of digestion.

Heart: its 2 chambers pump blood to the tissues of the body, including the gills, where carbon dioxide is released to the water.

Gills: absorb oxygen, which is transported to the various body tissues.

Esophagus: passage that food travels down from mouth to stomach.

Fins: help control the direction Bubbles moves in the water.

Intestine: helps digest Bubbles's food.

All these parts work together like a fine-tuned machine to help Bubbles maneuver and find food. They also help Bubbles the Fish avoid being caught by its predators. Think about that the next time you order fish and chips!

Check This Out:

Looking inside a fish is a great way to learn about internal organs. This is a bit smelly, but it's a lot of fun. So, plug your nose and dive in! If you can get a real fish with guts intact (say, after a fishing trip), carefully cut it open and identify its internal organs. Compare the inside of the real fish to the one you made.

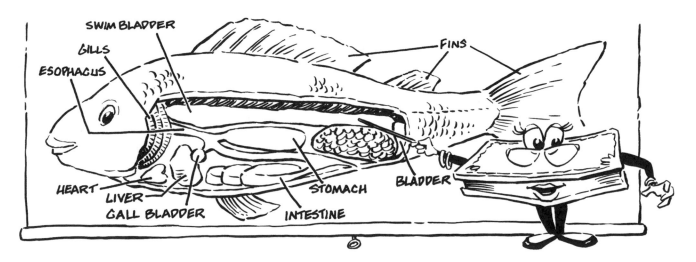

Toolbox: Classification

"Scientists like to be very organized, Dr. Lenslo. When biologists study plants and animals, they organize (or *classify*) them into groups similar to one another."

"That reminds me of where you live, Dr. Paige."

"Where I live?"

"Yes! The library. It's organized into different areas and sections to help people find what they want. Say you're looking for a book on tubas. You look tubas up on the computer and go directly to that area of the library. You don't have to look through every book. If you wanted to find out about other instruments, like piccolos, you could look on the shelves near the tuba books."

"Excellent example, my good Dr. Lenslo! While books are organized according to topics, living organisms are organized according to physical characteristics and behavior. Here's an example: Consider the killer whale. It belongs to the kingdom Animalia (animals); phylum Chordata (having a spinal cord at some point in its development); subphylum Vertebrata (having a spinal cord); class Mammalia (hairy and feed their young milk); order Cetaceans (whales, dolphins, and porpoises); suborder Odontoceti (having teeth); family Delphinidae (dolphins and killer whales); genus *Orcaella*; species *o. brevirostris*."

"Phew! What a mouthful! All that for a whale?"

"Sounds complicated, right? But it shows that everything in creation can be classified."

"Everything, Dr. Paige? Amazing!"

"Indeed, my magnifying friend. The reason? God used a pattern and design to put it all together. The pattern means there are lots of similarities among living things (like the design of cells). But each kind of organism is different from the others. And each member of a species is different from every other member!"

"Classy!"

"You try. Pick a drawer. Could be in your desk. Could be a dresser drawer. Pull everything out and lay it on the floor."

"Sounds like fun!"

"Come up with a classification system for the objects in front of you. You could group them into things you can write with, things to write on, and other things. Or, things you should keep, things you should throw away, and things walking around that should have been thrown away months ago!"

Whoo-oo Dunnit?

"My dear Dr. Lenslo, we have a mystery to solve."

"A mystery? Oh, I love a good mystery. Quick! Put on your detective's cap. There isn't a second to lose!"

"Now wait just a minute. Wouldn't you like to hear the facts first?"

"Oh. I suppose that would be the scientific way to approach the problem."

"Right you are. Here it is: Mrs. Higgenbottom reported the other morning that the population of goldfish in her pond had dropped drastically from what it was the night before. She assumed that the culprit must be a local bird. But she read in the paper that there had been a break-in at the bird display of the local zoo which resulted in the escape of a number of species. She looked for clues to determine which bird might be the guilty suspect.

"This is what she found: There were small white and black feathers lying around the pond. Upon closer inspection, she found an intermittent trail of feathers leading to an 18-inch (40 cm) high opening in the fence. Mrs. Higgenbottom looked over the fence and noticed a travel brochure for Antarctica.

"We got a list of suspects and made a criminal line-up."

"All ready, Detective Paige. Here we go. Let's examine the facts, look at the suspects, and draw conclusions."

Ostrich

Approximately 8 feet (2.4 m) tall. Weighs up to 300 pounds (136 kg). Males—black and white, females—mostly brown. Eat plants as well as small animals.

Sea Gull

Range from 11 to 31 inches (27 to 80 cm). Most are gray and white; some have black or brown feathers. Eat fish, eggs, insects, earthworms, garbage, and shellfish.

Chicken

Range from 20 ounces to 12 pounds (567 g to 5 kg). Brown, white, black, and reddish-brown. Eat worms, insects, seeds, and green stuff.

Owl

Range from 5 to 28 inches (13 to 71 cm) in length. Most are brown; some are red or gray. Eat small mammals.

Hawk

Range from 10 to 20 inches (25 to 51 cm) long. Black, brown, gray, and some white. Eat living prey, from insects to amphibians to reptiles to mammals appropriate to their size.

Penguin

From 16 to 38 inches (41 to 97 cm). Black and white. Primarily eat fish.

Macaw

From 12 to 39.4 inches (30 to 100 cm). A variety of bright colors. Eat seeds and fruit.

Humming Bird

From 2.17 to 3 inches (5.5 to 8 cm) in overall length. Usually bright, glittering colors. Eat nectar and tiny insects found within flowers.

Did you guess the right culprit? (Answer on page 155.) While we've had a bit of fun thinking about whoo-oo dunnit, did you notice something about birds?

There are SO many different kinds, shapes, and sizes. Each one has a *particular role to play*. Some help to keep rodent populations under control. Others pollinate flowers as they go about drinking nectar. Still others help clean up the earth by eating scraps from other animals'

meals. Each one has a specific purpose. And God made sure each one was perfectly equipped for its job. He took care of all the details.

You have a specific purpose, too! God has given you gifts and talents to use for his glory. Why not let God help you soar on the wings he has designed specifically for you? Check out Isaiah 40:29–31.

Ostrich   Sea Gull   Chicken   Owl

Hawk   Penguin   Macaw   Humming Bird

Hide-and-Go-Seek Birdie

Some birds, like eagles and hawks, were created to soar high above the earth. Other birds, like the grouse (found around the world in the northern hemisphere, usually in woodlands), have limited flying ability. As a result, it is harder for them to get away when their enemies come around looking to turn them into grouse burgers. Fortunately, the color of their feathers allows them to hide when they stay still. One variety (the ptarmigan) changes color with the season. In the winter its feathers are pure white, allowing it to hide on the snow. In the summer it has grayish brown feathers so it can hide among the grass and rocks. Now that's coming well-equipped!

Many, many birds have been equipped with feathers of just the right color to help them stay safe from their enemies. *Camouflage* keeps them hidden. But camouflage is not only dull colors. Sometimes the best way to hide is to be really bright . . . if you live in a colorful place. That's why tropical birds, where there are so many wild-colored flowers, are brightly colored.

Now it's your turn to design a camouflaged bird!

What You Need:

- Non-hardening modeling clay (see our recipe on page 155) of various colors.
- 2 or 3 (or more) friends.
- A backyard or park.

What You Need To Do:

Each person should select a variety of colors of clay and make a model of a bird. Don't worry about it if you aren't particularly good at art. Your job is to equip your bird with the camouflage it needs to keep safe from its enemies. You are going to try to make your bird in such a way that you will be able to hide it somewhere (even in plain sight) without your friend being able to see it. (More on that in a minute.)

Once everyone has finished their birds, decide what the boundaries of your hiding area will be. Allow everyone 5 minutes to go and hide their birds. The birds have to be visible (they can't be covered with leaves). Once everyone has met back at your designated starting point, start the game. The goal is to try and find the other peoples' birds before they find yours. The winner of the "Creative Camouflage Corporation" award will be the one whose bird stays hidden the longest without anyone finding it.

What Do You See?

Once everyone's bird has been found, compare the winning bird to the other ones. Can you see why it stayed hidden the longest? Try redesigning your bird so it could hide in a different location than the spot you hid it the first time.

Check This Out:

Camouflage can work in any environment. Play the camouflage game inside. Do you have brightly-colored furniture? Curtains? Design a house-trained house-bird that won't be found by the unsuspecting guest.

These two birds are hidden on page 96. Can you find them?

Bird-watching

Now that you're a bit wiser about the ways of birds, go for a walk and see if you can spot some camouflaged birds. You might want to take along some binoculars or bird-watching glasses. Notice the behavior of the birds as well. Some will blend in with their surroundings but will also sit very still so as not to be detected. Also, see if you can spot any birds' nests. How are they camouflaged?

Try visiting a variety of different areas (woodlands, forests, seashores, meadows) to see how the camouflage of birds varies from one area to the next. If you or your parents have a bird book, use it to identify the birds you've been able to see. Keep a record.

It's a Bird, It's a Plane, It's SUPER Feather!

Birds have many types of feathers. Some are downy and soft, helping to keep the bird warm. Others, called *flight feathers*, are specifically designed to help them stay up in the air and maneuver as they fly. Flight feathers have rows of hair-like structures called barbs. These barbs hook together by means of tiny barbules. When you see a bird pecking and stroking its wing feathers, it's actually re-zipping the barbs together, keeping the feathers in good condition for when it flies.

Check this out to see how a bird's feathers help it fly.

What You Need:
- A wing flight feather (from a larger bird such as a duck or a goose). Don't try to take one from a live bird! Look on the ground in a park where ducks and geese hang out, or buy one at a fly-fishing shop. (One side of flight feathers is wider, with longer barbs, than the other.)
- A hand-held hair-dryer.
- A push tack.
- A stick (a wooden ruler will work).

What You Need To Do:
Pin the feather to the top of the stick so the side with the shorter barbs is down and the point of the feather without barbs is toward you. Wiggle the feather to make sure it moves freely on the tack. Turn on the hair-dryer and point it at the feather. Blow air at the feather from different angles. Flip the feather over and see how it behaves when you blow air at it.

What Do You See?
When the feather is in the normal position, it lifts upward as the air moves over it. Now imagine whole rows of these feathers working together to produce enough upward lift to carry the bird off the ground. It's amazing that such light structures can help provide a powerful enough force to keep large birds, like geese and swans, up in the air!

Check This Out:
Dip feathers in various liquids, such as water and oil. Test them like the feather described above. How did the water affect the feather's performance? How did the oil affect its ability to create lift?

Dem Bones, Dem Bones, Dem . . . Rubbery Bones?

What You Need:

- A cooking pot.
- A medium-size jar with lid.
- 1 to 2 cups (250 to 500 ml) white vinegar.
- Various chicken bones.
- Adult supervision.

What You Need To Do:

After a chicken dinner, collect the bones and put them in a pot. Fill the pot with water and put it on the stove. Bring the water to a boil, then reduce the heat, allowing it to simmer for about 1 hour. This will loosen the other tissues attached to the bones. Add carrots and other vegetables and season to taste.

Hold it! Wrong recipe. Where were we? Oh, yes. Turn the burner off and remove the pot from the stove. Allow the pot and its contents to cool to room temperature. Remove as much of the loose meat tissue from the bones as you can. Rinse them under running tap water and place them in a jar. Pour the vinegar into the jar until the bones are covered. Allow this to stand 3–4 days, then check the bones. See if they are more flexible than when you put them in the vinegar. If not, allow them to sit for several more days. The larger the bones you use, the longer it will take to see the results.

What Do You See?

In healthy *bones*, minerals (mostly calcium) are taken up to help strengthen the bones. If a creature doesn't get proper nutrition so that not enough calcium is being obtained, the bones will start losing calcium, causing them to become weak. The bones in vinegar show the dramatic effect of calcium loss in bones.

Bird bones work best with this experiment because they are thinner (and therefore have less calcium) than other animals' bones. In fact, birds have some hollow bones specially designed for flight. This allows them to get off the ground more easily. God made sure birds' bones were adapted specifically for flight!

Up, Up, and Away!

Two important properties must be working together in any bird or plane that flies: balance and lift. Balance is necessary so that a bird's *flight* is not lopsided. Imagine if one wing were heavier than the other. If the bird did get off the ground, it might end up flying around in circles!

Lift has to happen for a bird or else it will have to content itself with strutting around like an ostrich. Try the activities on these pages to get a better idea of how these properties affect whether or not something will fly.

In the Balance

What You Need:
- A glass or cup with some drinking water in it.
- A golf ball-sized piece of non-hardening modeling clay (see our recipe on page 155).
- 2 identical forks.
- A toothpick.

What You Need To Do:
Roll the clay into a ball. Imagine you can see the numbers of a clock around the edge of the ball. Insert the prongs of the forks so that one of them sticks out at 4 o'clock and the other at 8 o'clock. Insert the toothpick at 6 o'clock. Now try to balance the "bird" by the toothpick on the edge of the cup.

What Do You See?
The forks *balance*! If you have trouble making it balance, try adjusting the size of the clay ball. Also, try putting the forks at different angles to one another. When you have it balanced nicely, you can drink out of the glass without disturbing your bird!

Check This Out:
Try this without the clay. Wedge a fork and a spoon together. Put the toothpick between the fork tines. See how little toothpick you can have protruding into the cup. Break off little pieces until the "bird" is balanced right on the lip of the cup. Looks impossible, doesn't it? The trick's in the balance.

Glide and Lift

What You Need:
• A piece of letter-sized paper.
• A small piece of adhesive tape.

What You Need To Do:
Fold the sheet of paper along one diagonal (from corner to corner—the sides won't match up evenly). About 1 inch (1 cm) from the edge, make another fold parallel to the first fold. Roll the folded edge once more and make a final fold. You have created a band several layers of paper thick.

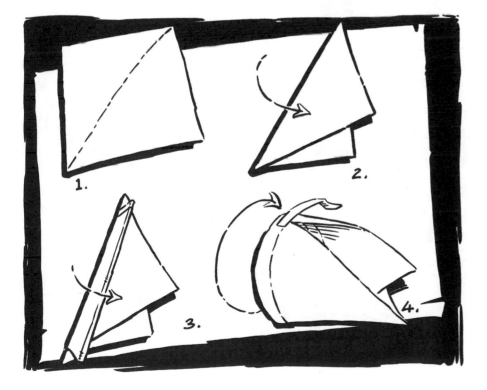

Shape this band into a circle, rolled edge facing out, and interlock the pointed ends. Secure the ends together with a small piece of adhesive tape. Put the glider into flight by throwing it with the rolled band facing forward and the tips of the "tail" on top. Try it from a balcony to see how it behaves from a higher launch site.

What Do You See?
It takes a bit of skill and practice to make something as simple as the glider you just made. When you flew it, you saw that it could fly only in a limited way. It could not start and stop without you going and picking it up after each throw.

Now think about all the different birds there are and the variety of ways they fly. Eagles unfold their wings and soar high into the sky, riding the air currents that rise from the ground. In contrast, a tiny humming bird beats its wings 25–75 times per second, allowing it to hover near a flower, moving in and out, as it drinks the life-giving nectar from the blossom.

Now take a look at your glider again. It doesn't begin to compare to the beauty and agility of the eagle or the humming bird. These are just two examples of the amazing design God has placed into the creation of each living thing.

Check This Out:
Design and make your own paper glider. Try to make one that flies the farthest, one that flies the highest, and one that does stunts (like a loop-the-loop). Does it come anywhere close to what a bird can do?

Winging It

Amazing discoveries about flight allow us to benefit greatly.

People have always been fascinated with flight. From Greek myths about guys making wings out of wax and feathers to the Wright brothers making the first motorized flights, people have wanted to soar with the eagles. While we will never be able to fly without the use of machines, God has given us the ability to study, learn, and creatively discover principles of his design. When our understanding of these principles is used constructively, the result is often incredibly useful machines and devices. The airplane is just one such invention. It all comes down to pressure and lift.

What You Need:

- A piece of letter-sized paper.
- Adhesive tape.
- 20 inches (50 cm) of string.
- A yard (meter) stick.

What You Need To Do:

Fold the paper widthwise so that one end overlaps the other by ⅜ of an inch (1 cm). Tape the two edges together. This is the wing. Pass the string through the opening between the folded sides of the paper. Attach both ends of the string to the yard stick, about 9 inches (22 cm) apart. Hold the stick straight out from you and turn it. Wave it around. Observe what the wing does.

What Do You See?

As the air moves around the wing, it goes more slowly across the bottom, bumping into the bottom surface. This creates pressure. The air going across the top passes over without hitting downward on the wing's surface. The result is lower pressure above the wing and higher pressure below the wing. The higher pressure pushes the wing up into the "space" the low pressure creates. This is what aeronautical engineers call *lift*. Lift keeps the plane up in the air while the engines push it forward. Birds and other flying things create lift when they fly as well.

"Flight is a really uplifting activity, Dr. Paige!"
"If you can handle the pressure, Dr. Lenslo!"
"It helps if you can wing it!"

Designed for Living Underwater

Like birds, fish are designed and equipped for their habitat. They have to be able to move to the surface of the water, to dive after food—and to avoid becoming food! How? They have *swim bladders* which help them adjust their buoyancy to the depth of the water. Oxygen and nitrogen are passed from the bloodstream into the swim bladder. If the fish needs to swim deeper, gas is reabsorbed from the bladder, deflating it. If the fish needs to rise to a higher level in the water, the bladder is inflated with the gases.

What You Need:
- An eye-dropper (this will be your "fish").
- 1 2-liter plastic soft drink bottle.
- A cup with water in it.

What You Need To Do:
Fill the bottle with water, leaving about 4 inches (10 cm) empty. Next, fill the eye-dropper ⅔ full with water by pressing on the bulb, putting the tip of the eye-dropper in the cup of water, and releasing the bulb. The air in the dropper is your fish's "swim bladder." Drop the eye-dropper into the bottle and put the lid on tightly.

Squeeze the bottle. Don't be shy! Grip the bottle with both hands and squeeze. Now release your grip. Watching what happens? Again. Squeeze. Release.

What Do You See?
The eye-dropper dives as you squeeze the bottle and rises as you release. Try it again, observing the water inside the eye-dropper this time. Let's go! Squeeze. Look. Release. Look.

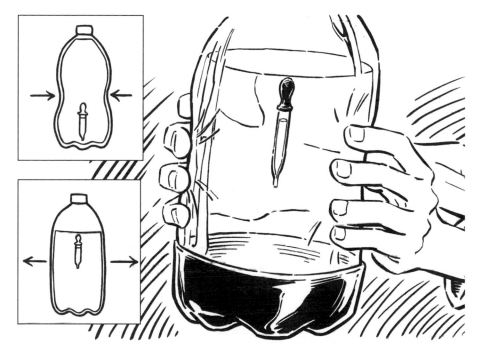

Notice anything? As you squeeze the bottle, you create pressure. This pressure pushes the water up the eye-dropper's glass tube, closer to the rubber bulb. The air in the rubber bulb gets squished into a smaller space, reducing its ability to float. The dropper sinks.

Try squeezing the bottle so the dropper neither sinks to the bottom nor stays at the top. This is the balance a fish has to achieve. It does this by adjusting the gas in its swim bladder: release gas from the bladder to dive; send oxygen and nitrogen into the swim bladder, inflating it like a balloon, to rise.

What a perfect design!

Sense Sent Scents

Pretend you're a salmon. How do you find your way back to the stream you hatched in? Some scientists believe salmon use their sense of *smell* to identify their home stream. See if you can find your "stream" by smell.

What You Need:
- Paper cups.
- Rubber bands.
- Some tissue paper.
- Several pieces of paper towel.
- A variety of scents (suggestions: garlic, fragrant herbs, perfumes, soaps, a pair of dirty socks, etc.).
- A felt marker.
- A group of friends or family members who want to smell real bad. (No, not people who want to stink; people who want to use their sense of smell!)

What You Need To Do:
Number the bottoms of the cups (1 for each scent). Place a sample of a scent in a cup. If it's in liquid form, pour a small amount of the scent on a piece of tissue paper. This will hold the scent in place. (Besides, you don't want perfume spilling all over the "stream.") To make it more challenging, place more than 1 scent in each cup. Place a piece of paper towel over the top and secure with a rubber band. Do this for each scent. Poke small holes in the tops of the containers. Assign each person 1 or 2 cups. Let them smell the sample (without looking in the cup) for 1 minute. Write down the names of the people participating and the number(s) on the cup(s) they're holding. Have them return the cups and leave the room.

Set the cups up around the room. Have the people come back in and, using the sense of smell only, find their home cup.

Check This Out:
If you like, you can "pollute" some of the streams by spraying room deodorizer or some other strong odor into the cups while the salmon are "at sea." See how this affects the fishes' ability to make their way home.

Salmon travel thousands of miles during their lifetime, but they manage to find the exact spot where their mothers laid the egg they hatched from. Incredible!

Seeing by Sound

What You Need:
- A super soaker water squirter or garden hose with sprayer.
- A variety of targets: some made from the same materials but different shapes and sizes, some the same shape but different sizes and materials, and some the same size but different shapes and materials. Examples: aluminum pie plates of different sizes, plastic lids the same sizes as the pie plates, different size baking pans, different towels.
- A blindfold.
- Several volunteer "dolphins" (parents, neighbors, unsuspecting passersby!).
- Optional: A clothesline or other cord suspended between two poles or trees.
- Clothespins.

What You Need To Do:
Ask your "dolphins" to wait where they can't see you setting up. Attach several targets to the clothesline with the clothespins. (If you don't have a clothesline, line your targets up along a fence or wall.) Leave at least 3 feet (1 m) between them. Fill the water reservoir of the super soaker and pump up the pressure.

Blindfold your first "dolphin" and stand him or her opposite the targets about 13 feet (4 m) away. Instruct the dolphin to "see" the targets by spraying the super soaker or hose back and forth.

Once your dolphin locates a target, have him or her try to determine its size, shape, and material. Do this for several targets. Test all your dolphins' ability to "see" with sound.

What Do You See?
Dolphins (like bats) see primarily by using sound, or *sonar*. Dolphins make almost non-stop clicking sounds near their blowholes. These sounds, with the help of an area in the dolphin's head called the oily melon, move forward through the water. When the sounds hit an object, they bounce back. The dolphin detects the reflected sound. And dinner is on! Dolphins also know where their fellow dolphins are so they don't crash into each other as they race through the water.

What you did with the super soaker/hose and targets was a model of this process. The stream of water acted like the clicking sounds the dolphin sends out. The sound of the water hitting the target is the reflected sound the dolphin detects.

Motion: Things That Oppose It

"I'll race you to the bottom!" challenged Dr. Lenslo. "And I'll win!"

"Don't be so sure about that," replied Dr. Paige, "I know a few sky-diving tricks to help me out."

"Hmmm. Well, let's go! On your mark, get set. Yeeeeeeeehaaaaaaaaaa!"

What You Need:
- A newspaper (the whole thing, still folded as if no one has read it).
- A square of toilet paper.
- A penny.
- An observer.

What You Need To Do:
Hold the newspaper flat in one outstretched hand and the penny in the other. Have your observer ready. Drop the paper and the penny at the same time. Ask the observer to see which one hit the ground first. Try this at least 5 times to be sure of your results. Do this same experiment using the toilet paper square and the penny. Then do it using the toilet paper square and the newspaper. Finally, place the square of toilet paper on top of the newspaper and drop the newspaper.

What do you think caused the results you saw?

What Do You See?
What you're observing are different *forces* in action. Gravity is the force that pulls all of the objects down to the ground. However, they travel at different speeds. Why? It all comes back to friction. The objects bump into air molecules as they drop. Lighter objects are less able to resist the force created by air, so they slow down. Also, larger objects, such

as the newspaper, bump into more air molecules (compared to the penny), so they slow down too.

When the toilet paper is placed on top of the newspaper and dropped, it falls at the same speed as the newspaper because the newspaper reduces the air friction it would normally experience.

Friction is a force that all creatures have to overcome (birds and fish included!) in order to move.

"That was cool!" exclaimed Dr. Lenslo, his head spinning.

"Yeah . . . real cool," replied Dr. Paige, holding her head and feeling a bit dazed. "Next time, let's remember to put a mattress down for a softer landing!"

Ladies and Gentlemen, Start Your . . . Soup Cans?!

Friction helps critters move. As they push themselves along, the force of friction pushes in the opposite direction, causing the critter to move in the direction it wants to go. Fish push against water. The water pushes back, moving the fish forward. Birds beat their wings against the air. The air pushes back and the birds dart about. A perfect arrangement that helps creatures move!

What about soup? Soup?!

What You Need:

• Several cans of soup (same size but different kinds).
• Self-stick notes.

• A 12 x 4-inch (30 x 10 cm) piece of thin wood.
• A small block of wood 1 inch (3 cm) thick.
• The floor or a clean counter top.
• Optional: A smooth, slightly slanted driveway.

What You Need To Do:

Set up a ramp by placing the block of wood under one end of the piece of wood. Lay one soup can on its side at the top of the ramp. Release it to roll down the ramp until it stops. Mark the spot where it stops with a self-stick note labeled with the type of soup. Go soup! Go! Do this for each type of soup. Repeat each roll 5 times to be sure you get the same results. If you're using your driveway, make sure your soup cans don't roll into the road.

What Do You See?

Really thin soups (such as chicken broth or consomme) cause very little friction as the can rolls, so they go quite far. Very thick soups, that come out of the can as one big lump when you open it (like creamy soups), roll very fast too because they stick to the sides of the can as if they were part of it.

Soups that have chunks of stuff in them, or are of medium thickness (like chicken noodle or tomato), tend to slow down. As the can starts to roll, the soup bumps against the sides and acts like a brake, causing friction between the soup and the can. Result? The can slows down.

Try canned fruit pieces. Have races!

Fishy Moves

Say you were a fish. What is it that lets you *move* easily through the water? What is it that lets you stop or change direction? Dive into this next activity and experiment to find answers. (Better do this outside where there's good drainage. Floods are out.)

What You Need:
• Non-hardening modeling clay (see recipe on page 155).
• A large, shallow basin or baking dish.
• A garden hose attached to a tap.
• A bamboo cooking skewer or stiff piece of wire (such as coat hanger wire).

What You Need To Do:
Make yourself a fish out of the clay. It can be imaginary or resemble one you're familiar with. (Remember Bubbles, page 92?) Fill the basin with water. Keep the hose running at one end of the basin, creating a gentle water flow through the basin. Push the skewer through the top of the fish's head so it comes out the bottom of the fish. (Don't worry, he won't feel it.) Lower the fish into the stream of water at the end of the basin opposite the hose. Holding the skewer, move the fish upstream. How easily did it move?

Now take your fish out and make some adjustments. For instance, make the head twice as big and really

blunt at the nose. Test your modified fish in the stream again. What happens? Try adding fins and making them stick out. Test it in the stream. Make the fins stick out on one side and lie flat on the other. Test it again. Bend the tail so that it points more to one side than the other. Test it again.

What Do You See?
A fish uses its muscles to adjust the position of its fins and tail to maneuver as it travels. By swaying its tail from side to side the fish can propel itself forward. The pointed shape of most fish allows them to dart through the water easily.

The *design* of the fish's shape and the ways it can move are perfect for the environment it lives in!

Sinking or Floating

Why do heavy things *float*? Think of a ship. It's made of steel, yet floats on the water. For that matter, think of a duck paddling along on a lake. Even though they weigh several pounds, they float on top of the water. It all comes down to the shape of the bird (or ship) and how much space it takes up in the water (its volume).

Shape It

What You Need:
- 2 sheets of aluminum foil exactly the same size.
- A large pan or bowl with water in it.

What You Need To Do:
Shape one sheet of aluminum foil into a boat (duck bottom!) shape. Crumple the second sheet into a very tight ball. Set the boat on top of the water. If it tips over, redesign it so it's balanced when it floats. Next, put the ball of foil beside the boat on the water. Let go.

What Do You See?
Even though the 2 pieces of foil are exactly the same size (and therefore the same weight), one sinks while the other floats. The next experiment will help explain this.

Overflow

What You Need:
- The materials from the last experiment.
- A pan the bowl can sit in that's larger than the top of the bowl.
- A measuring cup.

What You Need To Do:
Place the bowl in the pan. Carefully fill it with water right to the brim, but don't let it overflow. Gently place your boat on the water and allow the water to overflow. Measure how much water left the bowl by pouring the water in the pan into the measuring cup. Set the bowl up the same way again. This time, place the ball of foil on the water and let it sink. Measure the water that overflowed.

What Do You See?
The amount of water that overflowed was the same! Gravity tries to pull both to the bottom. However, because of the shape of the boat, its volume (space it takes up) is greater than the water it displaces. It floats!

Parting Shot

"Wow! Can you believe how many different creatures were added on the fifth day? And every detail taken care of!" marvelled Dr. Paige.

"You're not kidding!" answered Dr. Lenslo. "Amazing birds with brilliant colored feathers, some able to soar to great heights. The oceans, full of all sorts of creatures, some able to swim at great speeds while others are equipped to stay put in one place. Truly amazing!"

"Without exception each one has a special part to play in creation," Dr. Paige explained. "Each of their roles are unique, while at the same time they all play a part in helping each other survive. And the tiniest detail of what they each need to live has been taken care of. No exceptions. Scientists have discovered and learned incredible things (like how dolphins locate objects around them). And they keep discovering new things. What's more incredible is that God saw the whole picture of creation long before he spun our galaxy into place. What we see in the creatures of Day 5 is no exception to the rules and balance seen in other parts of creation."

"I believe there are lessons to learn from all this," pondered Dr. Lenslo.

"What are you thinking, my friend?"

"All things work together as the whole that God created and called 'good.' He takes care of the intimate details of the life of even the tiniest critters. Remember the mussel? And squid? Camouflage and swim bladders? All things shout that our Creator works in a planned and orderly fashion. He is truly awesome!"

"Precisely!" declared Dr. Paige. "Seems like Earth has gotten pretty full too. But God's plan was not quite finished."

"There's more?" asked Dr. Lenslo.

"Oh, you better believe there's more! As the curtain falls on this act of creation it's about to rise on another that will introduce the creature that would end up being the special focus of God's love."

"What's that?" asked Dr. Lenslo curiously.

"I'm not going to tell you and spoil the surprise!"

"Somehow I knew you'd say that! Let's see what God's final day of work would bring to the Earth, shall we?"

"I'm with you!" shouted Dr. Paige. "Let's go."

DAY 6

GOD MADE ANIMALS AND PEOPLE

Genesis 1:24–31: *Then God said, "Let the earth be filled with animals. . . ." And it happened. . . . Then God said, "Let us make human beings in our image and likeness. And let them rule . . . over all the earth. . . ." So God created human beings in his image. . . . God looked at everything he had made, and it was very good. Evening passed, and morning came. This was the sixth day.* (ICB)

"Lions, tigers, and bears, oh my!" Dorothy cried. "Toto, this doesn't look like Kansas! In fact, I don't even see the Yellow Brick Road!" Relax already, Dot. Even better than the land of Oz, we're going to explore the Garden of Eden in the early days.

Picture it: The sea is teeming with critters big and small, the land's covered with lush vegetation producing tons of fruit. But who's enjoying this unending fresh fruit stand? Well, flocks of birds. But, from the beginning, God saw an Earth populated by more than birds and fish. Enter the ferocious felines, chattering chipmunks, slithering snakes, ant-eating aardvarks, and gorging grasshoppers.

Even after these additions, God had one final member for excellent Eden. Our great great great . . . great grandfather, Adam. (Or was that Mr. Adam?) All creation was designed to bring glory and praise to God, but none more so than his final creation: people. We're unique among the creatures God placed in the Garden of Eden.

House Shopping in Crittersville

Creeping, crawling, scuttling critters are everywhere! Spiders spin their food-catching nets. Armies of ants locate and transport food in disciplined fashion. God made each for a specific purpose. He also designed them to live in areas that have what they need for food and shelter. Want to see these little critters choose the best *environment* for themselves?

What You Need:
- Critters looking for a new home. Beetles, ants, or ladybugs make great shoppers.
- A small jar (a baby food jar is perfect) to keep your critter in until you're ready. Make air holes in the lid, or cover it with material that lets air in.
- A cardboard box about 12 inches (30 cm) square, with flaps, if desired.
- A pencil.
- A ruler.
- Samples of grass clippings, sand, dirt, leaves, moss, small pebbles, etc.
- A circular object larger than the jar your critter is in.

What You Need To Do:
Find a little critter. Carefully put it in the jar, making sure it can get plenty of air. To test different critters, put each in a separate jar. Using the ruler and pencil, draw diagonal lines on the cardboard from corner to

corner. With the circular object, draw a circle at the point where the 2 lines cross in the center. Erase the lines inside the circle. In each of the 4 regions outside the circle, spread a different material that you collected. Cover as much of each region as possible. Once all 4 regions are covered, you're ready to let your critter go shopping.

Take the lid off the jar. Turn it upside down in the circle on the cardboard and let the bug choose one of the 4 areas. Note which one it moves into. Recapture the bug and, several minutes later, release it in the circle again. Do this 10 times, noting how often it goes into each area.

What Do You See?
The area the bug goes to most often has the conditions closest to those it would choose in the wild. God made it with the type of body for those conditions, and an appetite for the food found in that area. Perfect match! Every bug has a perfect home sweet home.

Help! I Need Somebody

Let's go! Back outside, on the double! Where's that tree you met back on Day 3? Found it? Great! You probably noticed it isn't the only thing living and growing there. Just like any of us can't live our lives without other people, the rest of creation includes many relationships between living things (plants and animals) and non-living stuff (like sunlight, soil, air, and water).

There are birds, fish, deer, bears, mushrooms, trees, grass, and many other creatures and plants. Each has a different role to play as members of its *ecosystem*. Ecologists (people who study the relationships among living things) classify members of an ecosystem by their role. The main parts of an ecosystem are the *producers* (anything that uses the sun for "food," like plants), *consumers* (creatures that eat plants and creatures that eat animals), *decomposers* (things that break down the dead remains of things that were alive), and *non-living stuff*.

But it's not just one big feeding frenzy. Critters provide important services to one another. Some help remove little critters that annoy others. For example, in Africa birds called cattle egrets ride around on bigger animals, like cape buffalo, wildebeests, or cattle! The egrets eat the ticks and flies on these animals. Or take tiny bacteria that live in digestive tracts (including ours). They do helpful things like producing vitamins and helping break down difficult-to-digest plant material. Their combined efforts make sure all life forms have energy, nutrients, and, in some cases, protection.

All these things are part of the ecosystem in that place. Ecosystems can get out of balance when things that harm some of the life forms (like pollution) are added to the system. That's one reason God called us to be caretakers of the Earth, to be careful not to pollute the world or waste the resources (plants and animals) he provided for us. We need each other!

What If?

What if one of the parts of the ecosystem pictured were removed? What if there were a disaster (like acid rain that can kill the plants)? How would it affect the other members?

Life on the Fly: Making a Fruit Fly Farm

Many critters' lives go in cycles. They start out in one form and metamorphose (change) into another, more mature form. This is one kind of *life cycle*. Fruit flies are good candidates for observing this cycle in action.

Some scientific experiments, like this one, take a while to set up and study. This will take half an hour to set up the experiment. In about two weeks you'll see the results. Be patient. It will be worth the wait!

What You Need:

- 2 medium jars, one with a lid.
- A kitchen funnel (large enough so its top is just larger than the mouth of the jar).
- 2 pieces of over-ripe banana or other over-ripe fruit.
- A piece of cloth, large enough to cover the opening of the jar.
- A rubber band.
- A magnifying glass.

What You Need To Do:

Place a piece of the fruit in each jar. Secure the lid on one jar. This will be your "control" (the comparison sample so you know the fruit flies that appear in the other jar didn't come out of the fruit; see page 125). Place the funnel, spout down, in the other jar. The funnel allows the fruit flies to enter the jar but makes it hard for them to leave. Once 5 or 6 fruit flies have been attracted to the jar, carefully remove the funnel and quickly pull the cloth over the opening so the flies don't escape. Secure the cloth with the rubber band.

What Do You See?

The fruit flies will (hopefully!) lay dozens of eggs on the fruit. With the magnifying glass, look to see if any eggs are visible. If you don't notice any within 2 or 3 days, try trapping some new fruit flies. Once you notice the eggs, watch them each day for changes.

The fruit flies will come out of the eggs as "larvae." The larva grows, shedding its coat (this is known as "molting"), then enters what will appear to be a lifeless stage (called the "pupa"). During this stage the fruit fly is developing into the mature adult.

When you're finished, carefully release your flies outside and clean the jars.

Little But Big

What You Need:

- Choose your favorite creepy crawler. Maybe it's a spider or an ant. Possibly it's a beetle or a centipede.
- A good-sized lump of non-hardening modeling clay (see our recipe on page 155).

What You Need To Do:

Use a very small amount of your clay to make a small model of your creepy thing (try to make it life-sized if possible). Remember, most creepy crawlers have really skinny legs. Once it's finished, lay it on its back (you know, the classic dead pose). Now use the rest of your clay to make a HUGE copy of your small critter. Make sure they're exactly the same except for size. Lay this large model on its back. Now, pick both of them up, one in each hand, and stand them right side up and observe what happens.

What Do You See?

Which one is standing? Probably the small one. You see, small creatures were designed to stand and move as small things. Once we make them really big they are just too heavy. Their bodies are just too big! Big creatures are specially designed with skeletons and muscles that allow them to move as big creatures.

God knew exactly what each creature would need to do and equipped each one for that purpose. That's a good thing too: We don't ever have to worry about meeting a 1,000 pound (500 kg) spider when we open our front door in the morning!

Think of all the different *insects* and bugs you've come across. There are fruit flies and horse flies and black flies. There are red ants and black ants. Annoying mosquitoes and beautiful butterflies. Bustling beetles and wandering wasps. Now, compare them to other animals, and what do you notice? They're all pretty small. But even though they're small, each of them plays an important role in creation. Many beetles and flies help pollinate flowers. Ants help by eating other dead bugs. Even though we find some of the behaviors of these creatures annoying, each was created with a unique purpose.

Fierce Lizards from the Past

Dinosaurs! Everybody loves them, but nobody has seen them. We know about them because of *fossils* we find in the ground. Fossils form when the remains of plants or animals are buried quickly, before they begin to rot (decompose). Over time, the actual plant or animal stuff is replaced by minerals that are dissolved in water in the ground. Scientists who study fossils (paleontologists) try to reconstruct the skeleton of the dinosaur. (You may have seen an example in a museum.) Quite often, though, some parts are missing. So the paleontologists have to guess what the missing parts would be like, based on what they've studied in other fossils. The pictures of dinosaurs in books and movies are the closest images artists can come up with based on what the scientists know. Who knows, Tyrannosaurus Rex might have been bright pink or had green and orange stripes!

What You Need:

- An aluminum pie or baking pan.
- Non-hardening modeling clay (see our recipe on page 155).
- Things to make fossils of: twigs, seashells, chicken bones, leaves, etc.
- 3 cups (750 ml) plaster of Paris.
- A container for mixing the plaster.
- 2 cups (500 ml) water.
- A stir stick.
- Toothpicks.

What You Need To Do:

Cover the bottom of the pan about ½ inch (1 cm) deep with modeling clay. Think of this as the mud your living things fell into long ago. Firmly press the objects you've chosen into the clay and remove them. Mix the plaster of Paris and water in the mixing container. Pour the mixture over the clay. This acts like the minerals in the ground water, replacing the actual living stuff that was buried. Allow to dry. Remove the pan and scrape away the clay. Carefully, like a paleontologist, scrape the clay out of any tiny cracks using the toothpicks.

What Do You See?

What can you tell about the objects that used to be in the "rock"? You can tell the shape and size of the objects, but not the color.

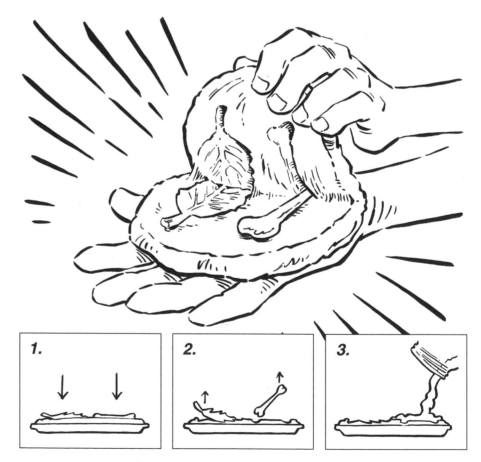

Solar Critters

Reptiles are animals that have a unique problem: They can't keep themselves warm. They have thick, dry skin, usually covered in scales. This helps to keep them from drying out, but it doesn't help them stay warm. Unlike humans and other mammals, reptiles are what is called *cold-blooded*. They rely on the sun's heat for warmth. They actually can't get going in the morning until their bodies warm up enough so they can move (and you thought *you* had a hard time getting out of bed!). This limits where they can live in the world. That's why the farther you go away from the equator, the fewer kinds of reptiles you find.

Try this to help you think about things that need heat to move.

What You Need:
- A pan or pot with a lid and a handle.
- 2 tablespoons (30 ml) cooking oil.
- ¼ cup (75 ml) popcorn kernels.
- A stove top.
- A pot holder or oven mitt.
- Adult assistant.

What You Need To Do:
Put the pot on the stove burner. Pour the oil into the pot. Turn the burner on to medium-high heat. Allow the pot to warm up for a couple of minutes. Test the oil to see if it's hot enough by dropping 1 kernel into the oil. When it pops, the pot is ready. Pour the rest of the popcorn kernels into the pot. Put the lid on the pot.

Using the pot holder to hold the lid on, shake the pot back and forth on the burner until you hear the popcorn popping. Remove it from the heat and see what happens. When the popping stops, move it back onto the burner and continue shaking it until the popping sounds can be heard. Remove it from the heat.

What Do You See?
Just like the popcorn has to have an external heat source to keep popping, reptiles require heat from the sun to be able to move and live. You'll never run into reptiles at the winter Olympics!

Oh! Better eat the popcorn!

Do YOU Know Your Wild Animals?

Check out the lists below. One lists the names of *wild animals* from around the world. The other describes them. Can you match the creature with its description? (Answers on page 155.)

1. African elephant
2. Orangutan
3. Jaguar
4. Bengal tiger
5. Praying mantis
6. Kangaroo
7. Boa constrictor
8. Chameleon
9. Tarantula
10. Gorilla
11. Polar bear
12. Koala

A. Parts of southern Europe, Africa, and the Middle East. Up to 12 inches (30 cm) long. Bug eaters (most insects and spiders). Solitary.
B. Forested regions on Borneo and Sumatra. Up to 200 pounds (90 kg), and 4 feet (1.2 m) tall. Mostly vegetarian. Also eat some insects and eggs. Solitary.
C. Forested and grassland regions of northern India and Bangladesh. Up to 575 pounds (175 kg), and 36 inches (90 cm) tall. Meat eaters (wild boar, monkey, and buffalo). Mostly solitary.
D. Most warmer parts of the world. Up to 12 inches (30 cm) long. Meat eaters (insects and spiders; larger ones eat frogs and birds). Solitary.
E. Hot grassland and forested regions of Africa. Up to 1,200 pounds (540 kg), and 10 feet (3 m) tall. Vegetarian (up to 500 pounds (225 kg) per day). Family groupings.
F. Desert areas of Australia's interior. Up to 200 pounds (90 kg), and 5 feet (1.5 m) tall. Vegetarian (grass and leaves). Live in herds.
G. Forested regions of central South America. Up to 250 pounds (110 kg), and 30 inches (75 cm) tall. Meat eaters (mammals, fish, frogs, and turtles). Mostly solitary.
H. Forested coastal regions of eastern Australia. Up to 26 pounds (12 kg), and 24 inches (60 cm) tall. Vegetarians (eucalyptus tree leaves). Solitary.
I. Forested regions of Central and South America. Up to 20 feet (6 m) long. Meat eaters (mammals and birds). Solitary.
J. Most warmer parts of the world. Up to 10 inches (25 cm) wide. Meat eaters (insects, lizards, frogs, snakes, and birds). Solitary.
K. Forested regions of central Africa. Up to 600 pounds (270 kg), and 6 feet (1.8 m) tall. Vegetarian (fruit leaves and tender stems). Sociable groupings.
L. Southern edge of the arctic ice cap. Up to 990 pounds (450 kg), and 5 feet (1.5 m) tall. Vegetarians and meat eaters (seals in winter, vegetation in summer). Mostly solitary.

Enzymes: Helping Out in Living Things

Animals' cells contain chemicals which are used to make other chemicals the body needs. Some of these chemicals are poisonous to the animal. They need to be changed into non-poisonous chemicals. Unfortunately, the reactions that form these new chemicals are often too slow. But God knew about this before he created anything. He designed some substances, *enzymes*, to speed up chemical reactions. Enzymes do this in living things without getting used up or changed themselves. That means they can be used over and over. Want to see it?

What You Need:

- A bottle of 3% hydrogen peroxide solution (you can purchase this at any pharmacy). Hydrogen peroxide can bleach clothing. Be careful. Wear a bib apron or old clothes and rubber gloves.
- A small piece of fresh liver (available at any grocery store butcher shop).
- 2 medium jars with lids.
- 2 wooden splints (thin wooden coffee stirrers work well).
- Matches.
- An adult.

What You Need To Do:

Pour ¾ cup (200 ml) hydrogen peroxide into each jar. Cut a piece of liver 1 inch square (3 x 3 cm). Place the liver in one of the jars. Put the lids on both jars and watch what happens. The jar without liver is your control (see page 125).

What Do You See?

The bubbles you see forming are oxygen. The reaction is changing the hydrogen peroxide into oxygen gas and water. Did you see any bubbles in the jar without the liver?

Hydrogen peroxide will, over time, break down into oxygen and water, but it happens very slowly. Liver contains the enzyme *catalase*, which speeds up the reaction.

Check This Out:

Test for oxygen. Have your adult helper use a match to light the wooden splint. Open the jar with the liver and have your helper blow out the splint, so there are red embers visible, and put the splint in the top of the jar. Don't touch the liquid.

What happens? The wooden splint re-ignites, showing oxygen is being formed. Try the splint test on your control jar. The splint doesn't re-ignite because the oxygen is being produced so slowly.

Digestion and Other Body Systems

Dr. Lenslo and Dr. Paige are about to chart the unexplored region of the *digestive tract*. They'll begin at the mouth of Subject X. They'll be transmogrified to fit into the Gastrolooker Exploration Module (GEM). The module is equipped with acid shields and will allow passage undetected. Good luck!

"Shhhhh, Dr. Lenslo! He's sleeping."

"I know! Listen to him snoring. When his mouth opens we'll maneuver the GEM into position to start our mission. Let's go!"

"Look at all the teeth! Careful! We don't want to accidentally get crushed," Dr. Paige said nervously.

"Not to fear, my bookish friend. The GEM can withstand incredible impact. Flip on the vision screen wipers. This guy is making a lot of saliva. He must be dreaming about food! A nice big banana split or a big plate of spaghetti . . . I'm starving!"

"Let's move on, Dr. Lenslo. Uh oh, sensors say we're being forced deeper into the oral cavity. We're riding a wave! Subject X is starting to swallow. Flip on the illumination units."

"You mean the lights, O learned one?"

"Of course! Look! The passage is narrowing. We're being pushed downward."

"Sensors indicate we're in the esophagus. It connects the mouth to the . . ." WHUMP! ". . . stomach. Boy, that was a rough landing."

Byoooop! Byoooop!

"RED ALERT, DR. LENSLO! Engage acid shields! We've entered an intense field of hydrochloric acid. I'm also reading the presence of partially digested food."

"All this squeezing and heaving going on is making me nauseous. There's a narrow passage ahead. Looks like a doorway. It's opening for that partially digested food. Let's speed up and go through, Dr. Paige. Faster!"

"We made it. Take a reading, Dr. Lenslo. Substances are being dumped in from other smaller openings."

"The GEM sensors identify these as digestive juices from the liver and pancreas. We're in the duodenum. Soon we'll detect food molecules being sucked out of the passage."

"There, Dr. Lenslo! Thousands of finger-like projections are attracting the food material. Let's speed ahead . . ."

"The passage is getting wider. The finger-like projections have been replaced by outward bulges, and there's a lot less liquid in here," Dr. Lenslo exclaimed.

"We're in the large intestine. Let's forge ahead. There's got to be a light at the end of this tunnel."

"There's a lot of garbage in here, Dr. Paige. It's moving toward our destination. I see a light ahead!"

"There's an opening, Dr. Lenslo. We've successfully completed our mission! Well done, my adventurous little buddy!"

How Long Is the Digestive Tract?

Let's make a model of the digestive tract and see just how far Dr. Lenslo and Dr. Paige had to go to complete their mission. Scientists use models to understand what they're studying. This model will show you just how long the digestive tract is.

What You Need:

- A small reclosable plastic bag.
- A tube from a roll of paper towel.
- A bread bag.
- A 20-foot (6 m) garden hose or thick piece of rope.
- A 5-foot (1.5 m) vacuum cleaner hose.
- Duct tape.
- A small travel or gym bag.

What You Need To Do:

Start with the reclosable plastic bag. This is the mouth. Cut a hole in one corner of the bottom. Tape one end of the paper towel tube (the esophagus) to the edges of the hole. Tape the other end to the top opening of the bread bag (the stomach). Make a small hole in the bottom of the bread bag. Tape it to one end of the garden hose (the small intestine). Tape the other end of the garden hose to one end of the vacuum cleaner hose (the large intestine).

Now, starting with the vacuum cleaner hose, stuff the digestive tract into the travel bag (the abdominal cavity). Keep going until the bread bag is in the travel bag, leaving the paper towel tube and the "mouth" sticking out. Having a bit of trouble fitting it all in? The digestive tract is made of very flexible materials which allow them to be packed into a small space.

Oxygen In, Carbon Dioxide Out

Breathe in, breathe out. In. Out. Pretty easy, isn't it? We don't even have to think about it, and we keep on *breathing*. Do it again. In . . . Out . . . In . . . Out. Ahhhhh! Fresh air. Our *lungs* were created for two main reasons: to allow our bodies to take in oxygen from the air and to allow our bodies to get rid of the carbon dioxide produced when we use energy molecules in parts such as our leg muscles. Check this out.

What You Need:
- A 2-liter soft drink bottle.
- 2 balloons, one large and one small.
- 2 rubber bands, one large and one small.
- Adhesive tape (duct tape works best).
- A ballpoint pen tube.
- Non-hardening modeling clay (see our recipe on page 155).
- A 12-inch (30 cm) piece of string.
- A pair of scissors with pointed tips.

What You Need To Do:
Using the scissors, cut off the bottom part of the bottle as shown. Keep the top half. Attach the small balloon to one end of the ballpoint pen tube using the small rubber band. Push the balloon end of the pen tube through the mouth of the bottle. When half the pen tube is through, seal the mouth of the bottle with the clay. Cut the large balloon in half with the scissors. Stretch it across the bottom opening of the bottle. Use the large rubber band to help hold it in place. Now tape the middle of the string to the center of the stretched balloon.

You're ready to test your model. Pull on the string, stretching the balloon.

What Do You See?
What happens inside the bottle? You should notice the small balloon inflating. The small balloon represents your lungs, the pen tube your trachea (or wind pipe), the inside of the bottle your chest cavity, and the large balloon your muscle called the diaphragm. When the diaphragm relaxes, the cavity gets smaller, forcing air out of your lungs due to increased pressure. When the diaphragm and other chest muscles contract, the chest cavity gets larger, causing the lungs to inflate due to the decreased pressure.

Take Your Breath Away

How much air do you think your lungs can hold? One liter? Five liters? Here's a device that will allow you to find out. It's called a *spirometer*.

What You Need:
- A large jar with a lid.
- A measuring cup.
- A bowl or basin.
- A 3-foot (1 m) piece of tubing (e.g., a piece of garden hose).
- Masking tape.
- A felt marker.
- An assistant.

What You Need To Do:
Pour 2 cups (500 ml) of water into the jar. Attach a small piece of tape to mark the height of the water. Continue adding 2-cup portions of water and marking the height of the water after each addition until the jar is full. Put the lid on the jar. Fill the bowl halfway with water. Turn the jar upside down and stand it in the bowl of water. Carefully remove the lid and insert one end of the tube into the jar, without letting any air get into the jar. You are now ready to measure your *lung capacity*.

Take a deep breath. Come on, you can take a deeper breath than that! Try again. That's better! Now, blow into the tube as hard as you can and keep blowing until you can't blow anymore. Feeling a little dizzy? Take it easy, then. Maybe even sit down for a minute. Now, check how much the level of the water has changed.

What Did You See?
When you blew air into the jar, it forced water out. Your lung capacity equals the volume of water you forced out of the jar by blowing in the tube. Get some of your friends and family to try it out. See who has the greatest lung capacity. Your lung capacity will depend upon how old you are, how big you are, and whether you are a girl or a boy.

Eden Olympics

Let the games begin! We're at the Edendome athletics complex to witness the games of the very first olympiad. Competitors and spectators have gathered from every corner of the Garden to be part of this historic event. Who will jump the highest? Run the fastest? Smell the best? The first heat of runners is approaching the starting blocks. It seems we're short one competitor. Hey! You there. No, don't point to the guy next to you. YOU! Come on out here. You might be a medal contender.

What You Need:
- Your running shoes.
- Athletic clothing appropriate for the weather.
- A running track 100 yards (100 m) long.
- Team-mates to compete with.
- A stopwatch or a wrist watch with built-in stopwatch.
- Measuring tape.
- A container of something smelly with the lid on.
- A CD or cassette player.

What You Need To Do:
100-Yard-Dash Event. Record each person's time.

Long-Jumping Event. Record each person's jump.
Smell Event. Stand 15 feet (5 m) behind your competitors. Take the lid off the smelly container. Tell them to raise a hand as soon as they smell something different. Time this.
Jumping-Straight-Up Event. Find a smooth wall. Have each person jump straight up and touch as high up the wall as possible. Measure how high each person touches.
Hearing Event. Slowly raise the volume on a CD player. Ask the competitors to raise a hand as they hear the music. Record the volume level.

What Do You See?
The results are in. The winners are on page 155.

How did you measure up? Feeling a little defeated? People aren't nearly as well equipped for doing the things these creatures do with such ease. But on the intelligence scale we're off the chart! We were created above all the others to have fellowship with God. That's a record no other creature will ever be able to hold!

Toolbox: Controls in Scientific Experiments

"It's important in any experiment to use proper controls, Dr. Lenslo."

"Are we talking about remote controls?" Dr. Lenslo inquired.

"No, not this time. Controls allow a scientist to know what has actually changed during an experiment. After the scientist has performed an experiment, the results can be compared to the control so that any changes can be determined."

"Hey! Like the closed jar with the fruit inside when we were farming fruit flies!"

"Exactly. And the non-livered jar when we were looking at enzymes. Controls are important for getting accurate results and understanding what our experiment shows us," Dr. Paige explained.

"Let me see if I understand. If I were to test which of 3 glass cleaners cleans my lens the best, I would mark off my lens into 4 equal areas. One of the 4 areas I wouldn't clean. Then I would clean each of the 3 other areas with a different cleaner. I could then compare the cleaned areas to the one I didn't clean to see which cleaner works the best. Am I on the right track?"

"Not only are you on the right track, you're riding the right train as well!"

"I love trains! Can I operate the controls?"

"Not this time, Dr. Lenslo. But when you do any experiments in the future, be sure to think about the controls you will need to use."

"What if the experiment is to test the remote control that controls a train? What kind of controls would I use?"

"I think you've lost me, but probably very controlled controls."

"Oh . . ."

"Anyhow, Dr. Lenslo, when doctors are testing new medicines they will give the real medicine to some people and fake medicine to a control group. That way they can see if the real medicine actually helps or not."

"Are they allergic to trains or something?"

"Okay, so the train just left the tracks . . ."

The Heart's Blood

Heartbeat and Pulse

Lub dub. Lub dub. Your *heartbeat*. It beats without your thinking about it—pumping blood to every part of your body, supplying you with oxygen and nutrient-rich blood every minute of every day. The blood picks up waste materials from your body tissues and transports them to the organs that remove them from your body. The blood also takes carbon dioxide from your tissues to your lungs so you can breathe it out with every breath. Your brain tells your heart when it needs to pump faster, like when you go for a run or play a game that requires a lot of energy.

Is there a doctor in the house? Make your own stethoscope.

What You Need:
- 2 kitchen funnels.
- A 3-foot (1 m) piece of tubing (such as garden hose).

What You Need To Do:
Insert the tip of the first funnel in one end of the hose. Do the same with the other funnel at the other end. Place one funnel over your heart and the other over one ear. Hear anything? If you can't, move the funnel on your chest until you do.

What Do You Hear?
The first part of the heartbeat (the "lub") is the sound of the valves opening and closing as blood returns to the heart. The second part (the "dub") is the valves closing as blood is pumped away from the heart.

There's another way to detect your heartbeat: your *pulse*.

What You Need:
- A marble-sized piece of non-hardening modeling clay (see our recipe on page 155).
- A toothpick.

What You Need To Do:
Roll the clay into a ball and insert the toothpick part way in. Find your pulse on the inside of your wrist. Attach the ball of clay at your pulse point with the toothpick pointing straight up.

What Do You See?
You should observe the toothpick moving to the beat of your heart. Lub dub. Lub dub.

Veins and Valves

Your *circulatory system* consists of your heart and all the blood vessels throughout your body. Vessels that take blood away from the heart are called *arteries*. When arteries are near the surface of your skin, you can detect a pulse (such as the spot on your wrist). The pumping of the heart keeps the blood moving through the arteries.

Vessels that return blood to the heart are called *veins*. Once the blood reaches the veins it isn't forced along by the pumping of the heart. Instead, the veins are squeezed as the muscles nearby expand and contract. Blood could collect in the veins if it weren't for the help of some structures called *valves*. Valves are located at various points along the veins. The valves allow blood to move in one direction only: back to the heart.

What You Need:
- Your one arm (or that of an adult assistant). Wait! Leave the arm attached!
- Your fingers on your other hand (leave these attached too).

What You Need To Do:
Locate one of your veins on the inside of your forearm. They're the blue-looking lines that run along your arm. (If you can't find one, try the back of your hand.) We want to show that the blood is moving up your arm towards your shoulder (and then to your heart). Make a tight fist with your hand on the arm you're testing. Starting near your elbow joint, run your middle finger down the vein 2 inches (5 cm), applying a small amount of pressure. Now slide your index (pointing) finger away from the middle finger, applying slight pressure. Keeping your middle finger in place, raise your index finger. What do you notice? Now put your index finger back in place and raise your middle finger. What happens?

What Do You See?
When you raise your middle finger blood continues to flow toward the heart. But when you lifted your index finger, blood that had already moved past that point didn't flow back down the arm. Valves in the vein prevented it from doing so.

Our Amazing Brains

Want to see how big your *brain* is and how it feels?

Brain in a Bag

What You Need:
- 1½ cups (375 ml) instant potato mixture.
- 2½ cups (625 ml) hot water.
- 2 cups (500 ml) sand.
- A bread bag (be sure it has no holes in it).
- A wooden mixing spoon.
- A twist-tie.

What You Need To Do:
Pour the ingredients into the bread bag. Stir thoroughly with the wooden spoon. Tie the top of the bag with a twist tie, releasing any air from the bag before closing it. Mold the bag into the shape of a brain.

What Do You See?
How does it feel? This model weighs what a real brain does (3 pounds or 1.35 kg). Get creative. Make the brain's grooves (fissures).

Remember the Eden Olympics? As humans, we aren't the best when it comes to the different functions you tried. However, a way we are unique and special compared to all the other creatures is our brains. We can think and reason in ways animals can't. Although animals can learn to do certain things (like the tricks you teach your dog), they can't create and imagine the way humans can. Part of that is due to the size of our brains, but mostly it's the structure.

Bagel Brain

What You Need:
- A bagel (or donut).
- Your index finger.
- 6 dinner napkins spread out and stacked on top of one another.

What You Need To Do:
Take a small chunk out of the bagel, just big enough for your finger to fit in. (So, what does brain taste like?) Stick your index finger into the slot in the bagel. Now lay the napkins over the top of the bagel.

Your index finger is the size of the brainstem. It's responsible for your basic survival responses. The bagel represents the brain's limbic system. This controls your emotions. Finally, the stack of dinner napkins represents the cortex. A human cortex takes up 85% of the brain. This is what really makes us different: It allows us to reason and think logically.

Ouch! Making a Point

Can you imagine what it would be like if you didn't have the *sense of touch*? You wouldn't be able to tell the difference between things that are rough and things that are smooth. Things that are hot would seem no different from things that are cold. If you stubbed your toe—Youch!—you wouldn't know it. If you picked up something burning hot, you wouldn't be able to tell. Your sense of touch is like a built-in alarm system that reports to your brain when your body comes in contact with things—in particular, things that might cause damage to you. Different parts of your body are more sensitive than others.

Match the Mark

What You Need:
• 2 ballpoint (or washable felt) pens of different colors.
• A blindfold.

What You Need To Do:
Blindfold the person you're going to test. Using one of the pens, mark a spot on the skin of your subject. Hand the person the other pen to mark where he or she thinks you touched. Measure how close the two are to one another. Try other parts of the body. The more sensitive the skin is, the easier it is for your subject to put a dot close to or right on the dot you put on him or her.

One or Two

What You Need:
• 6 paper clips.

What You Need To Do:
Unfold the paper clips and form them into "U" shapes. Make sure the 2 tips are even with one another. Adjust them so that one has its tips $\frac{1}{16}$ inch (2 mm) apart, another $\frac{1}{8}$ inch (4 mm), and then $\frac{3}{16}$, $\frac{1}{4}$, $\frac{5}{16}$, and $\frac{3}{8}$ inch (6, 8, 10, and 12 mm) apart. Blindfold your volunteer. Gently poke the person's skin with the tips of one of the paper clips. Ask the person if he or she feels one or two points. Try each of the paper clips and record the person's response to your question. Less sensitive skin will detect one point for most of the paper clips.

Hearing

Our sense of *hearing* is an amazing thing. It allows us to communicate when we're having a conversation with someone. It allows us to enjoy wonderful works of music and the beautiful sounds of creation when we walk through a forest or along the seashore. On a more practical level, our ears act as an early detection system for dangers that might be nearby (or even far away). Depending on the direction a sound comes from, it will reach each of our ears at a slightly different time. This doesn't mean we end up hearing two garbled-up sounds.

The difference is so small we don't notice it. But our brains do. The brain can then tell what direction the sound is coming from. Can you trick your sense of hearing?

What You Need:
• 2 plastic kitchen funnels.
• 2 1-yard (1 m) pieces of garden hose.
• 2 assistants/volunteers.

What You Need To Do:
Attach a funnel to one end of each of the pieces of hosing. Blindfold one of your volunteers. Hand him the other two ends of the hoses and have him put them gently against his ears. DO NOT jam the hoses into his ears. Holding the funnels in different directions, have your other assistant make noises in various parts of the room. As she does so, ask your blindfolded volunteer to guess (by pointing) which direction the noise is coming from. Move the funnels to different positions before each noise.

What Do You See? (Hear?)
Noises approaching us from one side of our head will reach the ear on the other side of our heads slightly later than the first ear. Our brain interprets the sounds we get from both ears so we have a sense of what direction the noise is coming from. Think what it would be like if you couldn't detect the direction a sound was coming from? Just one more way God has equipped us so we're protected but also able to enjoy the beautiful sounds of his creation!

Drum Solo

What You Need:

- A cereal (or soup) bowl.
- A piece of plastic food wrap.
- $\frac{1}{4}$ teaspoon (10 ml) of dried herbs (thyme works great!).
- A stereo or ghetto blaster (preferably one on which you can control the treble and the bass).

Note: Be sure you have your parents' permission to use the stereo. If you are not sure how to operate the system, ask one of your parents to assist you.

What You Need To Do:

Stretch the food wrap over the top of the bowl. Pull the wrap tight so that the surface is as smooth and wrinkle-free as possible. Sprinkle the dried herbs on the plastic surface covering the bowl. Place the bowl directly in front of one of the stereo speakers. Play some music and watch what happens.

What Do You See?

You should notice the dried herbs jumping up and down as the plastic surface vibrates with the music. Try different types of music at different volumes. Also, adjust the treble and the bass settings and see how that affects the behavior of the herbs on the "eardrum."

The *eardrums* in your ears respond to sound the same way the stretched plastic film does. As the air molecules are vibrated by the sound, the vibrations travel through the air and into your ears. The eardrum vibrates according to the type of sound being heard. Lower-pitched sounds (such as a man's bass voice or an electric bass guitar) are the result of longer wavelengths that cause bigger vibrations. Higher-pitched sounds (such as a woman's soprano voice or a flute) are a result of shorter wavelengths that cause smaller vibrations. These vibrations, with the help of a few other structures in your ear, are converted to electrical signals which are then communicated to the brain by nerve cells.

So the next time you think you hear drums playing in your head, it might just be your ears playing a drum solo. That, or maybe you should turn down your stereo!

Smelling Flavors

Much of what we *taste* actually depends on our sense of smell. Ever noticed that, when your sinuses are plugged, like when you have a cold, food doesn't seem to have as much flavor? Check it out.

What You Need:
• Various food samples (10 or more), preferably with fragrant smells.
• A spoon.
• A volunteer.

What You Need To Do:
Blindfold your subject. Have him hold his nose. (Make sure he keeps it plugged, but remind him not to squeeze so hard he makes his nose hurt.) Using the spoon, drop one of the food samples on his tongue. Ask him to tell you what he's tasting. See how many of the foods he can correctly identify without using his nose.

What Do You See?
Most flavors we think we enjoy as tastes are actually smells. Your sense of smell depends on special areas in your nose called *olfactory nerves*. There is a lot that scientists are still trying to find out about the sense of smell. They believe our brains can tell different smells from each other by a process that starts with chemicals from the food entering the cells near the olfactory nerve. It's even believed that it's the shape of these molecules that's detected. This information is sent to the brain via the olfactory nerve.

When you plug your nose, you prevent the delicious aroma of the food from entering it. As a result, you will not "taste" the food as you should. So, the next time you don't like the taste of something you're eating, politely say, "Pardon me while I excuse my nose from the meal!" Then plug your nose and chow down. It'll taste better. It will, at least, taste less.

Check This Out:
Cool samples of the same foods in the fridge for about an hour before testing them on your volunteer. See how temperature affects the flavor of foods.

Say Aaaaaaaaaaah!

Your *tongue* works along with other sites in your mouth to detect different flavors in your food. Three different regions on your tongue are specially designed to detect the 4 flavors of sweetness, sourness, saltiness, and bitterness. Your taste buds are made up of specialized cells that detect the flavors of the food you're eating. The flavors have to be dissolved in liquid in order for them to be detected by the taste buds. The information about what your mouth is tasting is transmitted to your brain so that the food can either be enjoyed, if the flavor is good, or quickly spit out if it doesn't taste good. Blah!

Let's find out which flavors are tasted where.

What You Need:

- 4 eyedroppers (if you don't have these, you can use toothpicks).
- 4 cups, each with one of the following flavor liquids in it: lemon juice (sour), water with a teaspoon of salt dissolved in it (salty), water with a teaspoon of sugar dissolved in it (sweet), and coffee or tea (bitter).
- Masking tape.
- A volunteer.
- Paper and a pen.

What You Need To Do:

Trace the diagram of the tongue. Label each cup using the masking tape and the pen. Don't allow your volunteer to see which cup you use for each test. Have your volunteer stick his tongue out at you. Don't take it personally! Choose one of the cups of liquid and, using an eyedropper, place a drop of it on one area of his tongue. Ask your volunteer to tell you if he can taste the liquid. Make a note on your diagram. Keep placing drops on different areas of the tongue. Once you've finished with the first liquid, let your volunteer have a glass of water to rinse his mouth out (be sure not to accidentally give him one of your test liquids!).

Do the same test with the other three liquids. Check out the answer on page 155 to see if you were able to successfully map the different taste buds in your volunteer's tongue.

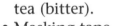

WHAT PART IS:
SWEET/SALTY?
BITTER?
SOUR?

Seeing through Things

Not all creatures *see* in the same way. Take a chameleon, for instance. These amazing little reptiles have eyes that can be rotated to look in different directions at the same time. This helps them keep a look out for things that would make a good meal and also keep an eye on things that might want chameleon for lunch. Many creatures, particularly birds of prey, have vision that's twice as sensitive as that of humans. For instance, an eagle circling high in the sky can spot a fish in a lake below and then dive at lightning speed to make a catch. None, however, has the special X-ray vision that humans have. You don't believe this? Before you decide for sure, try the activity below.

What You Need:

• A piece of letter-size paper.
• Adhesive tape.

What You Need To Do:

Roll the paper into a tube about 1 inch (2.5 cm) in diameter. Carefully hold the tube up to one eye with your left hand and look through the tube. Place your other hand next to the midpoint of the tube (halfway up) with your palm facing you. Keep looking though the tube with your left eye and at the palm of your other hand with your right eye. Do the same thing again, only switch the tube to your right eye.

What Do You See?

You've been able to observe a "hole" in the palm of the hand you were looking at. Why is that? Each of your eyes sees a slightly different image because of the distance between them. This would be a problem if it weren't for our brains. The image from each eye is communicated to the brain via the optic nerves. There the brain sorts out and combines the two images so that we see things clearly and with depth, rather than as two blurry images.

So, technically, humans don't have X-ray vision, but you almost thought you did when you tried this one, didn't you? Show someone else how they too can see through things!

Where Was That Again?

Eyes are amazing organs. Light from the objects we're looking at (such as the page you're reading right now!) travels into the eye and is focused by the lens. The focused light passes to the back of the eye (the retina) and is detected by special cells called rods and cones. These cells pass the image to the optic nerve, which transmits it by electrical signals to the brain. Having two eyes is essential for us to see things as three-dimensional images that have *depth*. If we only had one eye, we would be constantly bumping into things. Can you imagine people running around if they couldn't tell how close things were?

What You Need:
• A glass.
• At least 10 small objects such as paperclips, buttons, or pennies.
• A volunteer.

What You Need To Do:
Sit your volunteer at a table, with you seated across from her. Have her close both of her eyes. Place the cup on the table about 2 feet (60 cm) away from your volunteer. Have your volunteer open one of her eyes. Hold one of the objects up opposite her face, moving it around slowly.

Ask her to tell you when she thinks the object you're holding is above the cup. When she thinks it is, she should tell you to drop it.

Try this for each of the 10 objects. See how many she was able to accurately guide into the cup. Try it again, only this time move the cup farther away from your subject. Then, try it again with the cup closer to her. Finally, try it when she has both eyes open.

What Do You See?
When she had one eye closed it was more difficult for her to accurately predict when the small object was above the cup. God designed our eyes so they would produce an image that had depth. Our two eyes work together so we don't go around bumping into and tripping over everything!

Parting Shot

"What an incredible day!" Dr. Paige exclaimed. "Just when I thought there couldn't be anything more to add that was amazing or intriguing, God creates a whole pack of other creatures!"

Dr. Lenslo nodded. "What really amazes me is the fact that, no matter how incredible any of the animals are, none of them has a place as special as the one God gave people."

"Right you are, Dr. Lenslo! Remember the human brain?"

"Who could forget your brain bagel? I can't believe you made me eat the whole thing!" cried Dr. Lenslo.

"Oh! Tee hee! Sorry!" Dr. Paige giggled.

"I'm not sure I believe you, but carry on, just the same."

"No, really! I mean it! Where was I? Oh yes, the human brain. Humans are the only creatures with the ability to reason—to think about what they do and the choices they make rather than just react to whatever happens around them."

"Takes someone intelligent to make someone intelligent, don't you think? That shows God did it!" Dr. Lenslo declared.

"Exactly!" Dr. Paige agreed. "And humans were given a special quality no other creature has . . ."

"The ability to turn bagels into brains?"

"No, Mr. Lookalot. They were created in God's image! Nothing else in creation can make that claim," Dr. Paige explained.

"Why did God want creatures with that quality?" asked Dr. Lenslo curiously.

"He wants people to have a relationship with him. Also, as ones who carry his image, humans are called to be caretakers of the Earth."

"So people, especially those who know God, are expected to look after the Earth and care for the other creatures God made, particularly the other humans?" Dr. Lenslo asked.

"Right you are," responded Dr. Paige.

"It sounds like an exciting challenge!"

"It is, especially when you understand that God wants to walk with each person who takes up the challenge."

"Why wouldn't everyone jump at the chance to have a relationship with the God of the universe?" Dr. Lenslo asked.

"An excellent question. Can we come back to that in the last chapter?" asked Dr. Paige.

"Well, only if you promise not to make me eat any more of your experiments!" bargained Dr. Lenslo.

"Oh, all right. But the galaxy in a cup was astronomical . . ."

DAY 7

GOD RESTED

Genesis 2:1–3: *So the sky, the earth and all that filled them were finished. By the seventh day God finished the work he had been doing. So on the seventh day he rested from all his work. God blessed the seventh day and made it a holy day . . . because on that day he rested . . . from all the work he had done in creating the world.* (ICB)

Ah rest! Nothing feels better at the end of a busy day than to crawl between clean sheets on a comfy bed and drift off to La La Land. Your body slows down. Repair work is done to parts that might have been damaged. You're refreshed, ready to face the challenges of the next day. Is this an accident? Not a chance! God designed us and created rest and relaxation. It's his gift to us. Rest makes whatever else God has given us to do more enjoyable. In fact, a whole day of creation was set aside to emphasize God's gift of rest and what it represents.

It wasn't just God who rested. Everything he made, he designed to enjoy that same rest. Patterns of rest and renewal are visible throughout creation. Let's see how God's plan all along was for us to rest in the security of a relationship of trust with him.

Stressed Out about Being Stressed Out

Stress is talked about all the time. People talk about being "stressed out" or being "under a lot of stress." Let's try an experiment that demonstrates the original meaning of the word.

This is great to do as a contest between several teams (each with 2 to 3 members), but you can try it on your own too. Each group pretends they're engineers doing research. Your assignment is to design a structure that can be put under stress and still perform the function it was designed for.

Noodle Bridge

What You Need:
- 20 strips of uncooked dry fettucini noodles for each team (these should be as straight as possible).
- About 3 feet (1 m) of masking tape each.
- A stack of heavy books, similar in size and shape.

What You Need To Do:
Using only the strips of fettucini noodles and the 3 feet of masking tape, design a structure that will support the books at least 2 inches (5 cm) above the table top. [CAUTION: When you break the pieces of noodles, small pieces could fly out and hit you. Be sure to hold them away from you so that pieces don't hit you in the eyes.] Be creative in your design, but be sure it can meet the minimum requirements.

Once each team of engineers has its structure built, you're ready to test them. Place one book on top of the structure and see if it can support its weight. If it can, add another. Keep adding books until the structure collapses.

Carefully remove the books and go on to test the next team's structure.

What Do You See?
So, which design was able to hold up the most books? The books were being pulled down toward the table by gravity. The structure you built had to be able to push up with at least as much force as the books were pushing down with. What happened when the structure broke? Basically, it got "stressed out." Take a look at the remains of your creation. Can you see places where the noodles

broke after the books were placed on them? Those are the spots where the structure experienced the greatest amounts of stress. When the stress became greater than the noodles could handle, they snapped, causing the whole thing to come crashing down.

More Stressed Noodles

What You Need:
- A small package of spaghetti noodles (or part of a larger package).

- A paper cup.
- Enough pennies to fill the cup.
- A large paper clip.
- 2 tables of equal height (or two chairs that are flat at the tops of their backs and the same height).

What You Need To Do:
Put the 2 tables (or chairs, back to back) as close together as half the length of a spaghetti noodle. Lay one spaghetti noodle between the 2 tables. Make an S-hook out of the paper clip. Poke a small hole through the side of the paper cup just below the rim. Hook one end of your S-hook to the cup, through the hole, and the other end over the spaghetti noodle. Add one penny at a time into the cup until the noodle breaks. Do several trials using a new piece of spaghetti each time. Now try it using two pieces of spaghetti. Do additional tests, adding a piece of spaghetti each time, until you can hang the whole cup full of pennies on the bundle of spaghetti.

What Do You See?
When one noodle was expected to carry the whole load in the cup, it broke fairly soon. However, as more pieces were used together, the spaghetti "beam" became stronger and could support more pennies.

We've discovered that people experience stress in a similar way to noodles and other materials. Like noodles, when two people work together, they share the load and are able to do more than each could alone. We can help each other avoid stress by working together and helping one another out. A cup of pennies is much easier to carry if more than one noodle holds it up!

Sleepy Plants

Rest is such an awesome thing that even some flowers take naps. When winter comes, the sun shines less, the cold winds blow, and ice and snow blanket our gardens. Great weather for snowmen; not great at all for flowers. At such times you really can't blame a plant for closing down its food factories, tucking itself into the earth, and having a good rest. *Dormancy* is what a scientist would call it. You can call it anything you like, but what it is is rest.

Flowers like daffodils and hyacinths store some of the food produced during the sunny months in special stems called bulbs. The resting plant uses this food to keep it alive during winter and to begin growing in the spring. Although it's not the nicest thing to do to a sleeping flower, you can force it to wake up and act as if it were spring. It probably won't mind, and imagine a sweet smelling hyacinth blooming in your kitchen in the middle of winter!

What You Need:
- A hyacinth bulb. (Look for "pre-cooled" bulbs or put the not "pre-cooled" bulb in the refrigerator for a month.)
- A hyacinth glass, or something that looks like one (see the picture). Check your local garden center. Any narrow glass the bulb can sit on will do.

What You Need To Do:
Place the bulb in the glass. Add water to the hyacinth glass so it is just touching the base of the bulb. Place the container in the dark so it's encouraged to grow roots and add water as needed so the water level remains at the base of the bulb.

Within 6 to 8 weeks the roots will develop and the hyacinth bud will be about 1 inch high. Bring the bulb into the light—but not the bright sunlight which might burn the shoot. Your hyacinth will be convinced winter is over and should flower within 2 or 3 weeks.

Take some time to smell the hyacinth. Appreciate its beauty and design. Appreciate the designer who knew that resting was the best way to survive a cold winter.

Cocoon

There is a right time for everything. Everything on earth has its special season . . . (ICB)

You can read all about this sometime in Ecclesiastes, chapter 3. For now, realize that, like music, plant and animal life has rhythm. These *rhythms* tell the plant or animal the best times to grow, seek food, reproduce, and prepare for winter and rest.

On the seashore, animals move to the rhythm of the tides. Sea anemones and periwinkles close up while the tide is out but open when it returns. Crabs rest and are active according to built-in "clocks" that keep time to the tides' rhythm. For these animals, rest is the period between tides, a time to relax in the sand and wait for the next meal to be delivered. If you live near a seashore, take a walk at low tide and check this out.

Rhythms are also important in the nesting and migration of birds and the *hibernation* of some animals. Many hibernators have very accurate clocks that tell them to start hibernating at the same time each year. Hibernation is God's way of having an animal rest. It's a survival tactic to avoid the harsh weather and scarce food of winter.

Cooler nights and shorter days trigger the clocks within hibernators to start preparing for winter. Caterpillars respond to the rhythm of the seasons by spinning fall cocoons. During the harsh winter, inside the cocoon, the caterpillar turns into a moth. Only when the warm sun of spring returns does the moth hatch and fly away.

Want to see this rhythm in action? Go on a cocoon hunt.

What You Need:
• A glass jar.
• A lid with holes in it.

What You Need To Do:
The best place to search for cocoons is in a field after the weeds die in fall. Look for fuzzy cotton balls hanging from plant stems. Break off the stem with the cocoon still attached and keep it in a jar in your refrigerator until spring.

What Do You See?
When you take the cocoon out in spring, the warm days will act like an alarm clock and the moth should hatch from the cocoon, ready to start another cycle.

Dead Buds, or Are They?

Winter-time seems like such a dead time when we look at plants growing outdoors. Their leaves have fallen to the ground, and everything looks bare and lifeless. But is it? Put your coat on and go for a walk to look at some of these sleeping wonders.

Bud Watch

What You Need:
- Rose clippers (or something else to cut twigs).
- Different trees and bushes that have lost their leaves.
- An adult to help you cut twigs.
- A magnifying glass.

What You Need To Do:
Find different trees and bushes that have lost their leaves. Locate a branch with several *buds* on it and cut a sample twig. Take samples from several different types of plants. Carefully pull off the brown scales that cover the buds (these help protect them against the winter cold and from insects that might munch on them). Using your magnifying glass, observe what you have exposed.

What Do You See?
You should see tiny leaves folded up. Even though the plant you cut the branches from looks so dead, it's full of life, waiting for the warmth of spring when its winter rest is over and the tiny leaves will begin to unfold. Winter is a time of renewal, when the plant has completely shed its old coat from the previous summer and has begun the process of producing new leaves.

Waking Buds

What You Need:
- Same as the previous activity.
- A jar with water in it.

What You Need To Do:
Place the cut twigs in the water. If, after a week, there's no change, cut ½ inch (1.5 cm) from the end of the stems.

What Do You See?
You should notice the buds opening and the tiny leaves beginning to unfold. If the twig you have is one with flower buds on it, you may get tiny blossoms opening. You will now have the beginning of a beautiful winter flower display! Every time you see it, remind yourself of the awesome ways God has provided for his creation, including time for rest.

Toolbox: Conclusions

"As this is the last chapter in our book, this is a perfect place to talk about drawing conclusions," said Dr. Paige.

"Are you talking to me?" asked Dr. Lenslo.

"That would be a sound conclusion to make, considering that I am facing you as I speak and that you're the only other person in the room!" replied Dr. Paige.

"I like how you used pieces of evidence to come to that conclusion, Dr. Paige!"

"Evidence is very important. If, however, we have poor evidence, we aren't going to be able to make a very convincing conclusion."

"Can you give me an example?" asked Dr. Lenslo.

"Hmmm. Okay. Let's try a short activity. Take a look around the room. Any room will do. Just use whichever one you happen to be in. Slowly look around and try to explain what went on in the room over the past 24 hours. Look for evidence. Are there soft drink cans on the table and empty pizza boxes on the floor? Then probably someone had a party in that room. Is there a stack of books (some open and some closed) in the corner by some sheets of paper with notes on them? Probably someone was doing homework or getting information on a certain topic. However, we would have to try and find the people who were using the room to confirm what we think before we come to any conclusions."

"So we should never jump to conclusions too quickly before we know all the facts to help us form a proper conclusion, right?" asked Dr. Lenslo.

"Right. Nowhere is this more important than when we are making decisions in life. For those decisions we need to go to the best source of facts on how life works."

"Hmmm. A textbook on life?" Dr. Lenslo asked, puzzled.

"Exactly. The Bible. It is essential that we look in God's Word for clues about how we should live and act," Dr. Paige explained.

"Of course! With God's Word we'll always be able to know what the truth is. There are no hasty conclusions made in the Bible!"

Hormone Helpers

Ever see a cat meet a dog? Its hair stands on end, and its heartbeat races to catch up to its breathing. A dog means danger to a cat! You face dangers, too. You cross busy streets and friends jump out and surprise you. Danger is part of life. God designed life and gave us ways to deal with danger.

What You Need To Do:

Imagine you're cycling downhill on your way home. It's been a busy day of science experiments. You're tired and hungry. You pick up speed and head into the turn at the

bottom of the hill. Suddenly your front tire hits gravel. You get a sick, out-of-control sensation. You grip the handlebars tightly, give an expert flick of the wrists, and the bike straightens out. You're back in control!

What Do You See?

This 3-second incident saw a full-scale battle fought and won inside you! Your body's response to danger, the *fight or flight* response, was designed by the Creator to be lifesaving.

You don't have time to consciously do everything needed. The body's response to danger must be automatic: As soon as your brain sensed danger, it released an army of chemical messengers, *hormones*, into the blood. These stress hormones put all muscles on alert. The heart beat faster and harder. Sugar was dumped into your blood for emergency energy. More blood-clotting chemicals were made in case of bleeding. Your pupils dilated to let more light in. The bronchial tubes to your lungs opened wider for more oxygen. Sweat glands poured out aid to increase your grip on the handlebars. Blood from your largest organ, the skin, was sent to muscles, leaving you pale but lowering the danger of bleeding.

Five minutes later you probably feel that not much happened. You can rest. Rest is possible only because God designed a way for us to deal with dangers.

You might experience these same changes when you suddenly find yourself face to face with a spider. Next time it happens, pause and see if you can name the fight or flight responses that bring you back to rest.

Stress

The *fight or flight* response can save your life. Depending on choices you make, however, it might also keep you from rest or even make you sick.

What if there is no danger? What if you sit on your couch worrying about falling off your bike or failing a test? Does your body get ready to do battle even though you're safe? Yes. Lying in bed or sitting on a couch doesn't mean you're resting. If you're worrying about being the best at everything, or always feeling in a hurry, then you're not resting. In fact, alarms are going off in your body to get it ready for danger. All of the hormones that would help you run from a real emergency now go to work even though there is none.

If you go through this danger preparation often, you're not living life the way God designed. Instead of a life of peace, you're living a life of stress. Remember what happened to the fettucini noodles when you added stress to them? They bent just a bit and then *crash*! The scary thing is that stress, when constantly added to your life, can lead to a crash as well. Constant stress is unhealthy. But *rest and relaxation* increase health.

Are you resting? Rate yourself on our Rest Test. Check each of the following that you've done in the last month:

- ❏ talked to God about a problem
- ❏ enjoyed mealtimes
- ❏ enjoyed school work
- ❏ had prayer times
- ❏ had Bible reading time
- ❏ took time alone to think
- ❏ talked to parents about a problem
- ❏ exercised
- ❏ talked to friends about conflicts
- ❏ laughed a lot
- ❏ had regular just-for-fun playtime (not TV or video games)

So, how did you do? If you checked more than 7 you're probably resting the way God made us to rest. Did you notice that resting can just be plain fun? The God who designed you for life wants you to experience it at its best.

Take time to talk to him. Rest in him. Check out what God's Word says about rest:

- Psalm 37:7
- Proverbs 19:2
- Isaiah 26:3
- Matthew 11:28
- John 14:1–2
- Philippians 4:6–7

Now I Lay Me Down to Sleep

God made *rest*. Rest must be good. To find out how good, you may want to try going without for a night. Check with your parents first, however, since making sure you get your *sleep* has always been one of the ways they've shown their love for you. Once you have their permission, why not organize your sleepless night as a WAKE-A-THON? Talk to your friends, make up a pledge sheet, and see if you can get a few sponsors to support your scientific research. Look for a good cause for the money.

Now, if you're going to be awake for a few extra hours, you might as well make them productive. You can't just sit around watching TV all night. No way, that's too close to actually resting. You'd likely fall asleep halfway through the night. Turn your WAKE-A-THON into a WAKE-A-GAME-A-THON or a WAKE-A- . . .

Hold on now. Sounds like fun, but where is the science in this? How are we going to know what effect going without sleep has? You could go by how you feel the next morning. But what if one of the effects of going without sleep is to turn your brain into mush? You can't trust the conclusions of a scientist with a brain made of mush.

Better to get some non-WAKE-A-THON observers, perhaps an adult or two, who would be willing to observe you before and after the experiment. Here's what they should observe:

What You Need To Do:

In early evening, when you're still fairly fresh from the previous night's sleep, have your volunteer observer pick any page from the telephone book and give you one minute to see how many phone numbers you can memorize. Once the telephone book is taken away, your job is to write out all the numbers remembered. We'll call this "the brain test."

Now, a test for your body. How about 10 push-ups, 10 sit-ups, 10 deep knee-bends, 10 jumping jacks?

As soon as your night without sleep ends, you must once again have your observer test your brain and body. It might also be interesting to ask your observer if she notices anything different about the fruits of your spirit. How much gentleness, kindness, and love do you show before and after the WAKE-A-THON?

Trivia:
Randy Gardner holds the record for the longest continuous period of time that a human has gone without sleep! For a science project in 1965, Randy managed to stay awake for 264 hours. That's 11 days and nights. Talk about a Wake-a-thon!

What Do You See?

Other scientists who have done tests on sleep tell us that your results will be pretty much like their own. Going without sleep makes your brain and body work less effectively. Sleep is an important part of rest. Your body needs it. Your brain needs it. While you sleep, your heart rate, blood pressure, and body temperature are all reduced. You might think of them as being *at rest*. (This is the opposite of the flight or fight response.)

It's your brain that benefits from sleep even more than

your body. Experiments on people whose sleep has been interrupted suggest that a brain that gets sleep is less likely to break down. Thoughts, feelings, and attitudes are all affected by your brain. The longer you go without rest, the less likely people are going to want to hang out with you. To put it bluntly, you become a grump.

All of this matters. If your brain, your body, and your spirit are all out of whack, then you're going to make mistakes in what you do and say. Not being able to memorize some phone numbers is no big deal. But lack of sleep sometimes allows us to think and say things that can hurt those around us. Don't get caught up in the idea that you have to cram as much into life as possible. The God who designed the Earth and the life on it also designed that life to rest. When you're tired, sleep.

Staying Cool

Life takes care of itself. Remember holding your breath in Day 2? How long did you hold it? Two minutes? Three? Fact is, your body isn't about to let you stop breathing. At some point it says "Enough of this!" and forces you to gulp air. Your body talks to itself. Rob it of oxygen and every part knows. The blood tells the brain. The brain tells the muscles. The muscles make you breathe. Even the pain you feel is a signal to your body to stop doing what it's doing and get on with life.

Scientists call the results of such cooperative behavior *homeostasis*. "Homeo" means "same" and "stasis" means "standing still." Together they suggest something (your body) at constant conditions, or what we might call rest—your body working just as God designed.

Think about changes you go through in a day: sleeping, waking, lying still, running, becoming warm and cold. The environment around you changes. Yet it's super important that the environment inside you never change. Enter homeostasis: No matter what change the world throws at you, inside, where it matters, you're at rest. Test it.

What You Need:

- An oral thermometer.
- A watch.
- An adult partner.
- Exercise clothes.
- A pencil and paper to record your results.

What You Need To Do:

Get an adult to help take your temperature. Write it down with your breathing (how many breaths you take in a minute) and heart rates (see Day 6 for finding your pulse).

Do 20 minutes of exercise. Without resting, repeat and record the measurements. Check the appearance of your face, neck, and shoulders. After 20 minutes of rest, repeat the measurements.

What Do You See?

The exercise caused your body to heat up and your heart and breathing rates to increase. But not for long. Homeostasis took over, and soon things returned to normal (or below). Your body sent blood heated by exercise closer to your skin so the heat could escape. If you're fair-skinned, your face, neck, and shoulders may have turned redder. Sweating also cooled you.

The neat thing is that you didn't have to make it happen. Homeostasis is automatic. God designed it so you might rest.

Help, My Mouth Is on Fire!

Well, not really, but eating a jalapeno pepper sure makes your body think so. You're welcome to try a tiny piece of one if you doubt it.

What You Need:
- A jalapeno pepper (or something else really spicy).
- A big glass of water.
- Adult supervision.

What You Need To Do:
Take a tiny bite of the pepper (the size of the tip of your finger) and observe what happens.

What Do You See?
About 2 seconds after biting into the offensive fruit, special cells in your throat start screaming "Fire!" Your brain, being the boss, rings the alarm. Soon help, in the form of homeostasis, is on the way. Just as if you had been exercising for hours in the hot sun, your body responds to the munched pepper as if it were on fire. Once again, sweat begins to pour down your blushing face, your pulse races, and you begin to breath faster. But wait! Is your mouth or body really on fire? Is there really any danger here?

Not a bit! In a sense, the pepper has tricked your body into thinking there's danger of *overheating*. The fact is, nothing the pepper touches actually shows any increase in temperature. Your body, however, takes no chances—life is too important to take chances.

Put your body in any situation where it thinks it could be in danger and it's going to respond to protect itself. Every now and again something more violent than sweating is called for. Consider what happens when an invader such as dust or poison gets inside you. In response to dust, a sneeze produces hurricane-force winds (over 74 miles per hour) in your nasal passages and sends your heart rate skyrocketing. If you eat poison, coughing and vomiting use so many muscles in your chest and abdomen that you're left sore. Soon, however, the danger passes and your body rests.

You're safe again, thanks to a designer who knew you were going to come up against invaders. God took care of every detail so we would have all we need to be safe and healthy.

The Ultimate Cure for Worry

Our bodies and minds are complex things. (Remember digestion? Hormonal responses?) Things going on outside our bodies affect what goes on inside them. Some things we can control—what we wear, the food we eat, who we'll spend time with, how we'll use our time. Other things we can't control, but they're still part of our lives: the weather, illnesses, pop quizzes . . . When we think about these things we might worry. It's a natural response in humans! But, just as God planned for everything else, he provided a way to handle our worries.

What You Need:

- A pen.
- A notebook or journal.
- A quiet place to be alone, either in your house or outside.
- Your Bible.

What You Need To Do:

Find a quiet place where you won't be disturbed. If you go outside, be sure to let an adult know where you are (we don't want anyone worrying about you!). Read Matthew 6:25–34. Open your notebook and put the date at the top of the page. Below the date, list anything bothering you. Pray, asking God to take care of these things. (Worrying about things can't change them—giving them to God can.) Read Philippians 4:6–7. Let God give you the peace he promises there.

What Do You See?

Feel better? Think of the amazing experiments we've done that show the ways God designed things so all his creatures have what they need. He cares for you even more than them!

Prayer isn't something we use to get our own way. Through prayer we take our needs and worries to God. We ask him to show us what he wants us to do in the situation. You might have ideas about how God could answer your prayers. Don't be surprised if he has something different (and far better!) in mind. When you see your prayers answered, go back to your notebook and jot down how God provided for you.

God is interested in all of creation, and you're at the top of his priority list! We really can rest, knowing he has everything in our lives under control, including the things that worry us.

Trust Me!

Rest is important. So is *trust*. In fact, trust is a kind of rest. God designed us to be healthier and happier when we trust (especially when we trust him). Trust is the opposite of stress. Like stress, it shows in our bodies (remember our flight or fight hormones?). If we don't trust those around us, for example, we'll probably worry and might not sleep well. We have to trust our parents to look after us. We have to trust our friends too. It's important to know we can depend on them. Get a couple friends and try this.

What You Need:
- A mattress (or thick pillows you can lay out in the shape of a mattress).
- An adult to supervise.
- A carpeted floor.
- 3 participants.

What You Need To Do:
Stand one person at the end of the mattress or pillows, with his back to it. The others should stand behind him, about 1 foot (30 cm) away. The two people behind the volunteer should put their hands out ready to catch him. Have the volunteer close his eyes, cross his arms, and say "Ready," then fall straight back (without bending his knees or waist) into his friends' hands.

Move the two catchers back a bit and try again. Do it several times, but don't move the catchers so far back they can't catch the person falling.

What Do You See?
How did it feel? Worried your buddies might not catch you? Did they? (Fortunately, the mattress was there in case they missed.) You had to trust your friends not to let you down—literally!

"God is way more trustworthy than people!" Dr. Lenslo exclaimed.

"Indeed. He took care of every detail of our physical lives. Do you think he took as much care for our spiritual and emotional lives?" Dr. Paige asked.

"Of course! He had a plan for that too. He has a plan for EVERYTHING!"

"Absolutely! Through his Son Jesus' coming and dying for us, God took care of every single spiritual and emotional need we would ever have!" Dr. Paige declared.

"We just need to trust him! He never lets us down."

Parting Shot

"Hawwthk! Pshoooo. Hawwthk! Pshoooo."

"Dr. Lenslo . . . LENSLO!" shouted Dr. Paige.

"Uh? What?! Did I miss something? I was having the best sleep and an awesome dream!" Dr. Lenslo declared dreamily.

"It must have been about a sawmill! You sounded like logs being sawed," Dr. Paige chuckled.

"Verrrrry funny."

"It's good to see—and hear—that you learned the importance of rest from the things we tried."

"Actually, I was dreaming about God creating the entire universe knowing people would be the ones to really benefit from it all. Imagine! A God so powerful and intelligent, and yet so interested in tiny little humans on an itsy bitsy planet in one corner of the universe! That blows me away!" Dr. Lenslo exclaimed.

"You are so right, Dr. Lenslo, my friend! All the Days built up to the final Day, the day of rest. God designed cycles of rest for all creation. And us."

"But Adam and Eve sinned and ruined it all," Dr. Lenslo sighed.

"But we've seen how God planned for every detail of life. He also planned a way to bring us back to rest with him . . ."

"Jesus," Dr. Lenslo interrupted. "God sent his Son Jesus to pay for our sin!"

"Exactly! Jesus' death allows us to return to the rest God intended," Dr. Paige explained. "We can be at complete rest and peace. Our bodies rest as they work as God planned . . ."

"Our minds rest when we trust God each day," Dr. Lenslo added.

"And our spirits rest through being forgiven," Dr. Paige concluded. "Complete rest, like creation on the seventh day!"

"And all anyone has to do to get this rest is have a relationship with God by believing in Jesus and inviting him to be part of his or her life. It's so simple! Yet what God gives us is out of this world!"

"Right!" Dr. Paige exclaimed. "Aren't you glad we took the time to explore the days of creation? I'm more amazed than ever by our incredible God! Well, that's it for our look at creation. Any last thoughts, Dr. Lenslo?"

"Most definitely! Just because this book is finished doesn't mean there aren't more things to learn about God through his creation. Stay alert. Keep learning. Good-bye from this lab!"

"Bye," shouted Dr. Paige, "and keep observing for the unexpected!"

ANSWERS

page 34–35: Kittywampus "Facts"

If you wrote anything at all about the characteristics of Kittywampus, you fail. Sorry. Kittywampus, you see, is nothing more than your friendly neighborhood kitty-cat. The material that Dr. Paige presented had much that was true about cats, but it started off with something that was untrue. The Kittywampus skull was not the skull of an extinct animal because no such animal has ever lived. Check any dictionary, any encyclopedia, or any CD-rom and you won't find any mention of the beast.

Evidence is not evidence until it has been tested.

page 49: From Paper to Ping-Pong Balls

If you checked every item, you win the prestigious *Wood Detective* award. Each is made from trees or materials that come from various parts of trees!

page 53: Facts or Superstition

There's no evidence for any of these, and therefore they are superstitions rather than facts.

1. Toads, when in pain, can give off an irritating substance, but this substance does not cause warts. Warts are caused by viruses.

2. Dragonflies do not and cannot sting.

3. Tarantulas rarely ever bite, and when it does occur it is not serious.

4. The reflected light that comes from the moon is too feeble to have any effect on the plant factories' operation.

5. The dodo bird is extinct.

6. Usually mules are not capable of having babies, but there are a few cases on record in which they have.

7. No rule. Sorry. You should always be sure of what you're eating before you eat it. After all, look what happened to Alice in *Alice in Wonderland*.

8. Nice try, but on average boys are just as smart as girls, or, if you prefer, girls are just as smart as boys.

9. Up until a chap by the name of Galileo came along, everyone thought so, simply because someone important had said so. Problem was, no one bothered to actually try it until Galileo climbed the Leaning Tower of Pisa and made it happen. And that was the point of this little quiz . . . it's always better to test what people say before you decide it's a fact.

page 77: Things Affected by the Moon

Let's see how you did.

1. No! If you're standing on the moon, however, be sure your toothpaste tube doesn't go flying off into space.

2. While the World Wide Web does require us to "surf the net," this is not affected by the moon.

3. This won't be influenced by the moon, unless you're trying to do it by moonlight. Lakes don't experience the tides we observe at the ocean.

4. This is *believed* to be due to the moon's influence. However, there is no proof.

5. Bad hair days are not affected by the moon; they're unpredictable and most likely due to being rushed in the morning.

6. Yes? Correct! The high tide twice a day allows the creatures living in the *intertidal zone* to feed in nutrient-rich sea water.

7. Yes to this one too! Fortunately, the movement of the Earth's crust is very slight, so we don't have to walk through dirt waves twice a day!

8. No. The force of gravity that keeps us from flying off into space is caused by the Earth.

9. If you're a surfin' dude, you should be glad for the moon. The moon pulls on the Earth's oceans, causing large waves to form in the open seas and roll in toward land.

10. Although the space around the moon is a vacuum, this does not affect your Hoover®. Besides, the hose would have to be nearly 250,000 miles (400,000 km) long! (For more on vacuums, see Day 2, pages 30–31.)

page 81: What if . . . ?

- **If Earth were any closer to the Sun**, life would be wiped out by the sun's radiation.

- **If Earth's temperature were even a few degrees cooler**, the ice caps at the North and South Poles would grow, causing more heat and light to be reflected back into space, causing even more ice to form and a further drop in temperature.

- **If Earth's temperature were even a few degrees warmer**, more water and carbon dioxide would be released into the atmosphere, causing a greater greenhouse effect, which would cause Earth's temperature to rise even more.

- **If Earth rotated more quickly**, wind velocities would be so high that nothing could survive (such as is the case on Jupiter).

- **If Earth rotated less quickly**, the difference between daytime and nighttime temperatures would be too great to support life.

- **If Earth didn't have a planetary neighbor the size of Jupiter**, it would be struck about 1,000 times more often by debris from comets. Jupiter is $2\frac{1}{2}$ times more massive than all the planets in our solar system combined. We're talking monstrous planet! Because of its size, it attracts (or deflects off into space) a lot of the debris that would otherwise be attracted to Earth.

- **If Earth's moon were smaller**, there would not be enough of a tide to allow nutrients to be brought to the shore.

- **If Earth's moon were larger**, the effects of the tides would be too great, causing problems in coastal areas.

page 94: Whoo-oo Dunnit?

If you've arrested the penguin, then you've won the *Detective of the Year Award!*

page 118: Do You Know Your Wild Animals?

1. African elephant . . . . E
2. Orangutan . . . . B
3. Jaguar . . . . G
4. Bengal tiger C
5. Praying mantis . . . . D
6. Kangaroo . . . . F
7. Boa constrictor I
8. Chameleon . . . . A
9. Tarantula . . . . J
10. Gorilla . . . . K
11. Polar bear L
12. Koala . . . . H

page 124: Eden Olympics Winners

- **100-Yard Dash:** cheetah—traveling at speeds of up to 60 miles per hour (100 km/h), it could cover 100 yards in approximately 4 seconds!

- **Long Jumping:** 42 feet (12.8 m) by a kangaroo.

- **Smelling Something:** male Emperor moth, which can detect faint odors from 7 miles (11 km) away.

- **Jumping Straight Up:** 10 feet (3.1 m) by a kangaroo.

- **Hearing Something:** bats' hearing is at least 10 times more sensitive than that of humans.

page 133: Tongue Map

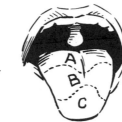

A = Bitter
B = Sour
C = Sweet
   and Salty

RECIPE FOR NON-HARDENING MODELING CLAY

What You Need:
- 1 cup flour.
- 1 cup water.
- ½ cup salt.
- 2 tsp cream of tartar.
- ½ tsp food coloring of choice.

What You Need To Do:
Mix all the dry ingredients together. Then add all the wet ingredients. Ask an adult to cook your mixture over medium heat for 3 to 5 minutes while you stir constantly. Knead your clay.

Store your clay in an air-tight container.

GLOSSARY

acid

a substance that tastes sour and has a pH of less than 7.

atmosphere

the envelope or blanket of gases that surrounds Earth.

base

a substance that tastes bitter and has a pH of more than 7.

carotene

an orange-yellow pigment found in carrots, squash, and other living materials.

chlorophyll

green pigment found in plants that is capable of absorbing the sun's energy during photosynthesis.

classification

a system for organizing organisms into groups with similar characteristics.

condensation

the process by which a gas or vapor changes to a liquid.

density

the mass of something divided by its volume.

ecosystem

a community of animals, plants, and bacteria that are all interrelated with each other and their physical environment.

elements

pure substances made up of only one kind of particle.

enzymes

complicated materials produced by living creatures that speed up chemical reactions without being used up.

fermentation

the splitting of complex sugars by living organisms to give carbon dioxide and ethanol.

glucose

a simple sugar that the body uses for energy.

glycogen

a form of glucose that an animal stores in its liver.

gravity

the natural force of stars and planets (like Earth) that pulls objects toward its center.

hibernation

resting through the winter.

homeostasis

keeping things constant within a living organism.

hormones

chemicals that act as messengers within the blood.

hygiene

things you do to stay healthy.

lift

the force that acts on a wing or airplane in an upward direction, against the pull of gravity, and helps the bird or plane fly.

mass
a measure of the amount of matter in something.

microscope
a scientific tool that allows you to see very tiny objects that otherwise would not be seen.

minerals
solid, pure substances that are found naturally in the earth and have a definite chemical composition.

molecule
two or more atoms combined to make one particle.

nutrients
a nourishing ingredient in a food.

optic nerve
the nerve that leads from the eye to the brain.

photosensitive
sensitive to light.

photosynthesis
the process whereby a plant uses the sun's energy to make food.

pigments
the colored chemicals in a plant that absorb the sun's energy.

properties
any observable fact that can be used to identify a particular material.

refraction
the bending of light.

retina
the innermost layer of the eye that detects light.

species
kinds or types of organisms.

spectrum
the series of colored bands (from red to violet) that light can be broken into.

starch
the storage form of glucose in plants.

transparent
something that allows light to pass through it without scattering it.

troposphere
the first layer of the atmosphere.

vacuum
a space empty of matter.

vaporized
changed into a gas.

volume
the amount of space something takes up.

xanthophyll
one of the photosynthetic pigments.

INDEX

Lightwave Publishing Inc.

Lightwave Publishing is a recognized leader in developing quality resources that encourage, assist, and equip parents to build Christian faith in their families.

Under the direction of Rick Osborne, Lightwave has been producing high quality materials since 1984. Among the more than 30 resources are the *101 Questions Children Ask about God series, The Singing Bible, Sticky Situations (the McGee and Me Game), The Adventure Bible Handbook, The Amazing Treasure Bible, The Quest Kids*

Study Bible and *Financial Parenting,* co-authored by Larry Burkett and Rick Osborne.

Lightwave Publishing offers a free newsletter called *Tips & Tools for Spiritual Parenting*. This newsletter helps parents with issues such as answering their childrens' questions, helping make church more exciting, teaching children how to pray, and much more. To receive a free one-year subscription, simply write to the address below or call **1-800-555-9884.**

Lightwave Publishing Inc.
133
800 - 5th Ave.,
Suite 101,
Seattle, WA
98104–3191

or in Canada

Lightwave Publishing Inc.
Box 160
Maple Ridge, B.C.
Canada V2X 7G1

You and your children are also welcome to visit Lightwave on the Internet at **www.lightwavepublishing.com**

Lightwave Publishing does not accept or solicit donations.